AGAINST THE TIDE

Rethinking What It Means To Make Disciples

George Alexander

AGAINST THE TIDE

Rethinking What It Means To Make Disciples

George Alexander

AGAINST THE TIDE

Rethinking What It Means To Make Disciples

by George Alexander

ISBN 978-0-9955601-1-6

Unless otherwise stated, all Scripture references are
from the *Holy Bible: New International Version* (NIV),
copyright © 1973, 1978, 1984 by the International
Bible Society. Used by permission of Hodder &
Stoughton.

Artios Publishing
13 Whinhill
Dunfermline
Fife KY11 4YZ
www.artios.org
mail@artios.org

Dedication

This book is dedicated in a general sense to the leaders and all the ministers who form Liberty Network International. In the days before that name appeared, the same people were known as Church Foundational Network. And even before that, many of us were part of Liberty Fellowship of Churches and Ministers, together with the others who still operate under that name. I include you all. Thank you for your warmth and welcome, from my first participation in the fellowship back in 1985, and through all these years to the present day. Thank you too for your continuing companionship and challenge.

This book is dedicated more specifically to Don Loose, my early teacher and still my friend. You first taught me about discipleship, and I am grateful for the grounding. It has helped me navigate in the waves and the winds of doctrine.

Like most of us, I learned and I followed, picking up on all the terminology as I heard it used, and growing accustomed to that usage. Over the last few years, I have been provoked to reconsider what the New Testament really says about discipleship, and particularly about *making disciples*. This book is the result. You may find it in some combination both provoking and annoying! My hope is that you will reconsider these matters along with me. To that end, I finally dedicate this book to all those who are willing to keep an open mind, and rethink what it means to make disciples.

George Alexander
January 2018

Contents

Introduction

It was the end of a large inter-church meeting in Dunfermline Abbey, under the banner of a movement of that time called "There Is Hope". I had been sitting about two-thirds of the way back to the right of centre, and my purpose was to make my way to the front to congratulate and encourage one of our couples who had been contributing some special music to the evening. The task sounded simple. What I had not expected was that everyone else in the building, or so it seemed, immediately stood up and made for the exits at the back, and home. They showed considerable determination. My journey to the front was slow and difficult. As I learned that night, measuring progress when travelling in a contrary direction to the crowd is a recipe for discouragement.

Some people are naturally strong swimmers. Others are not. As an experiment years ago, my wife Mary temporarily suspended the arm movements in her usual breaststroke. Using only her legs, she found to her surprise that she moved slowly *backwards*. No wonder her arms were tired!

Safe enough in a swimming pool, it may be a different thing in the open sea. Even the strongest of swimmers can get into trouble in some of the currents encountered within sight of the shoreline. For all their efforts, in a cross-current or a counter-current, it's easy to be swept off in an unintended direction. Even if safety is not an issue, moving against the direction of the current is hard work.

Why then, since I *know* all this, am I about to choose to do the equivalent of swimming against the tide? Why would I *do* that? It would certainly be easier to go with the flow!

I'm about to call into question some popular and widespread teachings in the area of discipleship. These teachings are very high on the value list and dear to the heart of many of my friends and colleagues. Unless I have a relational death wish, surely I must have a good reason for swimming against the popular tide in this way! The only reason I can offer is that these contemporary teachings and assumptions do not align with Scripture. But then surely that is reason enough.

As in any area, the danger always exists that we have taken up these discipleship teachings relatively uncritically, making assumptions that at first glance seem to be right. Yet assumptions can get us in trouble. I encourage you to read what follows carefully in order that we take time to check our foundation in this area and see whether these assumptions are all valid.

Some may dismiss or ignore my concerns without taking time to consider them, perhaps because of settled confidence, or perhaps because of closed-mindedness. There is little I can do about this, but it is disappointing. We owe it to each other and to Truth to be teachable. Some others may find my concerns irritating or annoying or even unsettling. Yet they will quickly forget them and revert to familiar terminology. This is also disappointing, although understandable. It is possible that some of my friends and colleagues will feel that my concerns are a betrayal of a distinctive that they have laboured to create. I certainly hope not.

My hope rather is that you will read these points and arguments with an open mind, and find in them a ring of truth that will cause you to re-evaluate some of your assumptions. Are we so sure that we are right? Might there be some points that we should adjust? Perhaps some of the very frustrations we have had with discipleship in practice are because we are pursuing some aspect or other that is slightly "off". In that case the irritation may prove helpful!

My own conclusion is that I'm challenging terminology rather than principle. I think, and I hope that you will agree, that our underlying principles are basically sound; but that some of the terms, and the verses we have tied them to, are not being used appropriately. And this difference matters. It is important for the sake of our understanding, for the sake of our obedience going forward, and for the longevity of the movement that we represent.

Having shared these concerns and ideas with several colleagues already, the response has been generally favourable. But in some cases, this has been mixed with a flustered and frustrated result, because they have realised just how central these concepts are to our conversation, and how different our language needs to be if these things are so.

That phrase leads me naturally to Acts 17:11, which words you will no doubt recognise:

> Now the Bereans were of more noble character than the Thessalonians, for they received the message with great eagerness and examined the Scriptures every day to see if what Paul said was true.

ONE

What Do We Often Hear?

Pastors sometimes despair of the Church because the people act in a way that is shallow or frivolous or immature. We want a people who are serious and holy and spiritual. And yet we so often see things that are worldly and unspiritual and fleshly. (We don't want to say carnal, although it means the same thing.)

Pastors may not admit to these feelings very loudly or very publicly, because we feel that if the people are not acting right, the problem may be to do with our preaching! But pastors do ask the questions: How can I get my people to behave themselves better? How do I get them to take Christianity more seriously? How do I get them to grow up? I'm glad they're Christians, but I wish they were better ones!

Some pastors find the answer where it surely lies, in the Gospel and the message of reigning in life. Others try to focus on external holiness and the rules of good order. Yet others try to foster obedience to God and His Word by strengthening their pastoral authority and seeking to hold their people accountable in a greater way. Much legalism and control have resulted from these approaches. Yet the problem persists.

One of the things that get the blame for this state of affairs is the long history of decisional evangelism. The evangelist in the large crusade, the evangelist in the market place and the evangelist working one-to-one with non-Christians are all concerned with individuals making a *decision* for Jesus. It may mean coming down to the front, or inviting Jesus into your heart, or praying the sinner's prayer, or all of the above—but the goal is to get them *in*. Once they are across the line—lost to found, unbeliever to believer, non-Christian to Christian, unsaved to saved, natural person to born again—the typical evangelist thinks his job is done and his responsibility finished. Now others should do the follow up.

This leads to many church members who are content to have their ticket to heaven. They have crossed the line from non-Christian to Christian, and can now presumably live their lives any old how, knowing that their ultimate destiny is taken care of. They will sometimes joke that they have sorted out their life assurance and their fire insurance, and now they are all set!

Their pastors will preach that they should live right, and they may comply, partly out of gratitude, partly out of fear, and partly on a just-in-case basis. However, there is typically very little vision or personal revelation in play. Thus even behaviour that looks okay is at best patchy. It's frustrating for the pastor.

Then the frustrated pastor is reading his Bible one day, and he comes across the words of Jesus in Matthew 28, "Go and make disciples of all nations." Something connects in his heart, and he says, "That's it! That's the answer. Jesus didn't call us to make *converts*, He called us to make *disciples!*"

Suddenly it seems obvious that the traditional model of the evangelist is in fact a model to make *converts*—and no wonder they are all over the place behaviourally. Jesus called us to make *disciples*, which immediately suggests shaping and forming and training. The very word *disciple* must surely be connected with and involve *discipline*. And that is exactly what the frustrated pastor has been looking for—a *disciplined learner*. He concludes that *discipleship* is the missing element in his Church, and begins to consider how to fix this omission.

The idea that Jesus calls us to make *disciples*, not just *converts*, has staying power. It sounds like a statement of simple truth, and somehow seems to say, "Why didn't I think of that before?" It is a statement frequently heard around many churches in these days.

Making disciples

The words about making disciples of all nations come from a section of Scripture at the end of Matthew's gospel, which today is almost universally known as the Great Commission. We hear it a lot when discipleship is being talked about.

> [18]Then Jesus came to them and said, "All authority in heaven and on earth has been given to me. [19]Therefore go and make disciples of all nations, baptising them in the name of the Father and of the Son and of the Holy Spirit, [20]and teaching them to obey everything I have commanded you. And surely I am with you always, to the very end of the age."
>
> Matthew 28:18-20

These are the final verses in Matthew's gospel. So we are told that Jesus' last words must be extra significant. His last words are surely our marching orders. We must be very careful that we obey these words and do not neglect them. The test of our faithfulness will be: when He finally returns, will we still be doing the things He told us to do? In particular, will we still be obeying the final instructions, these things most important, the very heart of our commission?

Jesus taught us to "make disciples". Did He model what He taught? Why, yes! He did many things as recorded in the gospel accounts, including preaching to the multitudes, healing the sick, casting out demons and raising the dead. But surely the overarching accomplishment of His earthly ministry was to recruit, train and invest Himself in twelve individuals in whose hands the whole project would be left after the Ascension. He certainly did make disciples, and the process took His whole earthly ministry, up to three-and-a-half years. For such a critical long-term process, He had to choose wisely and with the greatest of care. What would the early Church have looked like if He had had to restart the process after two years because the first lot went off the rails, and their replacements then denied the faith? Jesus modelled careful selection, patient formation and confident release at the right time.

Inspired by His example, we see a model for us to follow also.   We may be involved in many other things, but the central focus of our commission is to "make disciples," and so we too must select carefully and work patiently, investing ourselves in the right people for the eventual right time.

Whose disciples are they?

Rather than "making disciples," it is common in some contexts to hear the word *disciple* turned into a verb, so that we talk about *discipling* people. Someone may ask, "Will you disciple me?"   A positive answer to this request would be, "Yes, I'll disciple you." When used in this way, *discipling* really means processing, establishing, encouraging and training the person concerned to be a responsible, self-motivated, fruit-bearing believer; or in other words, a disciple.

This question, "Will you disciple me?" leads naturally to another difference of approach. The New Testament speaks of disciples of the Pharisees, disciples of Moses, disciples of John the Baptist, and of course disciples of Jesus.   One approach is to assume from this that there would also be disciples of Peter, disciples of Paul, and so on.   For this understanding, the phrase "make disciples" means *make your own disciples just like Jesus made* His *disciples*.   In other words, the disciples you make are *your* disciples, disciples of *you*.

The other approach is to understand that Christian disciples are all disciples of *Jesus* and Jesus only.   In this understanding, the phrase "make disciples" means *make disciples of Jesus*.   This is a fundamental and critical difference.   Unless we check and continually define terms, there is a great potential and a high likelihood here of us misunderstanding one another in either direction.

Making disciples who make disciples

Looking again at the passage Matthew 28:18-20, we often hear today that, according to a grammatical analysis of the text, the main imperative in this Great Commission is "make disciples," and that all the other phrases are incidental to this one. However it is clear by the nature of the process, and it is underlined by the incidental phrase, "teaching them to obey everything I have commanded you," that the Commission is cyclical. By this we mean that the disciples we make are themselves to make disciples, who in turn are also to make disciples, and so on. We often hear the summary phrase, "making disciples who make disciples," or sometimes the alternative, "making disciple-makers". The rolling and expanding nature of this should lead to a continual multiplication of the growth rate, and to exponential increase in the total numbers.

Some have taught that there must be significance to the use of the number twelve. Jesus raised up twelve. Twelve is the number of government, and government may have relevance given that the motivation of many frustrated pastors that leads them in this discipleship direction is a motivation to call people to *obey* the things of truth. With this in mind, some have taught that we each should work to raise up not hundreds, not scores, but specifically twelve. Then we work with those twelve as Jesus worked with *His* twelve. And all of our twelve themselves raise up twelve others. This is not so commonly heard today, but it has been popular even in recent years.

However, what *is* commonly heard today is the focus on making disciples. It's a new priority that sounds like it might be an old priority rediscovered—making disciples who make disciples. It is common today to hold this priority so strongly and centrally, that it becomes the litmus test of our validity in ministry. We may be doing ministry in other ways, and it may be fruitful to an extent. But if we are not making disciples who make disciples, then we are falling short biblically, and things need to change. And if we *are* making disciples who make disciples, whatever else we are *not* doing, at least we are fulfilling the heart of what we are fundamentally commissioned to do.

Associated with these emphases, although with a wider definition, is the word *missional*. If we are missional, we must be fulfilling the missions mandate Jesus gave us. But if we are not making disciples who make disciples, how can we be fulfilling His missions mandate? How then can we truly call ourselves *missional?*

Summary

Here are some phrases to summarise the things we often hear as mentioned in this chapter:

- The words of the Great Commission are the final words of Jesus.

- Jesus calls us to make *disciples*, not just *converts*.

- A disciple is a *disciplined learner*.

- The disciples I am making are my disciples.

- The goal of my life should be to raise up twelve disciples.

- During His earthly ministry, Jesus modelled the process of making disciples.

- A disciple is the end product of a process of *discipling*.

- The heart of the Great Commission is the imperative to make disciples.

- Since making disciples who make disciples is the process we are in, we should choose wisely whom we disciple.

- If I am not making disciples who make disciples, then I am falling short biblically.

These bullet points represent the chapter so far.

You may have been reading through this chapter in broad agreement with what has been said, and wondering exactly what tide I am swimming against.

I must take a pause before writing the next paragraph:

In the following chapters, I will call into question *every one* of these ideas. In fact, it is my contention that every bullet point, as expressed above, is incorrect in some way.

TWO

Laying The Foundation

If you want your house to last, don't build on sand. That is a very obvious statement that almost everyone can grasp and agree with. But still it is tempting to short-circuit the foundation-laying process and go straight to the more interesting or visible aspects of construction.

It's a powerful verse. Paul wrote to Timothy:

> *And the things you have heard me say in the presence of many witnesses entrust to reliable men who will also be qualified to teach others.*

> 2 Timothy 2:2

We identify in this verse four generations of Christian workers. First there is Paul, who has passed these things on secondly to Timothy, who is to entrust them thirdly to reliable or faithful men (really men or women), who will be qualified to pass them on fourthly to others. We can talk here of passing the baton, of reproduction of ministry, of a reproducible process. There's expansion here, and the possibility of the exponential increase that we mentioned in chapter one.

This passage has long been associated with the language of discipleship and making disciples. Many have linked it very strongly with the principles of discipleship. A quick look online reveals multiple associations and images, like:

2 Timothy 2:2 – The Plan of Discipleship, or

The 2 Timothy 2:2 Model of Discipling

But there is an obvious problem. The word *disciple* is not in the verse at all. Neither is it found in this chapter—or in this letter—or indeed in *any* of Paul's Letters!

The fact is that Paul does not use the word *disciple* at all.

So we could grab for this verse as an interesting and colourful and powerful verse that seems clearly to fit with the subject of discipleship and making disciples. We could make it part of our construction and combine it with other insights. But we would be building on sand. A link between discipleship and this verse is an assumption. The assumption may be correct or incorrect, but we have no way of knowing until we have taken the time to lay the foundation.

The foundation involves surveying the actual words involved, asking what they mean and seeing where they occur. This is what we will now do.

The word *disciple* in English means "one who professes to receive instruction from another; one who follows or believes in the doctrine of another; a follower, especially one of the twelve apostles of Christ." This, of course, is a noun; and the word is not usually considered to exist as a verb in current English. Now the English language meaning is interesting and informative as far as it goes, but it is limited for our purposes, since it is simply an appropriate translation of the actual New Testament word, which is Greek. The word *disciple* comes from the Latin *discipulus*, meaning "a learner or student or pupil". In chapter one, the similarity to the word *discipline* was noted, and sure enough *discipline* is derived from the same Latin term. Does this mean that *disciple* and *discipline* are linked terms and that a disciple is therefore a *disciplined learner?* No, it does not. The link applies in English, and possibly in Latin; but the New Testament is not written in English or Latin. It is written in Greek, and the Greek words for *disciple* and *discipline* are quite distinct.

The Greek word translated *disciple* is the word *mathetes*. (To be clear, this is the Greek word transliterated into our normal alphabet. The actual Greek word would look more like μαθητής.) The meaning of *mathetes* is "a learner or pupil". The word is derived from the verb *manthano*, meaning "to learn or understand".

There are two additional nouns to mention at this point. The first is the Greek word *mathetria*, which is the female equivalent of *mathetes*. It occurs only once, of Dorcas.

> *In Joppa there was a disciple name Tabitha (which, when translated, is Dorcas) ...*
>
> Acts 9:36

The second is the form *summathetes*, a fellow disciple, also found in a single occurrence.

> *Therefore Thomas, who is called Didymus, said to his fellow disciples ...*   John 11:16, NAS

Having dealt with the variants, *mathetes* itself occurs 261 times in the New Testament (using the Nestle-Aland Greek New Testament, 27th Edition, usually written as NA27). These 261 break down as seventy-two occurrences in Matthew, forty-six in Mark, thirty-seven in Luke, seventy-eight in John, and twenty-eight in Acts. The word *disciple* therefore does not occur in any of Paul's Letters, nor in the General Letters, or in Revelation. The word is no longer used after Acts 21:16.

In the Gospels, *mathetes* is used twelve times for disciples of John the Baptist (three times in Matthew, twice in Mark, four times in Luke and three in John); it is used twice for disciples of the Pharisees (once each in Matthew and Mark); and it is used once for disciples of Moses in John 9:28. The remaining occurrences all pertain to disciples of Jesus.

In Acts, all the occurrences, with the possible exception of Acts 9:25, use the word *disciple* or *disciples* exactly as we might say *believer* or *believers*. In fact, the New Living Translation translates almost all the occurrences of *mathetes* as *believer* or *believers* in Acts. We will come back to this observation in a later chapter.

[With regard to Acts 9:25, there are two views. Referring to those who helped Paul to escape, some translations render the phrase in question, "his followers" or "his disciples"; while others translate the idea as, "the disciples" (or "some of the other believers" in the case of the NLT).]

The word *discipleship*—which we hear and use fairly frequently—is not actually found in the Bible at all. (To say this is not to say anything negative about the idea of discipleship. There are many words that are important to us, and yet are not found in the Bible, for example *Trinity* and *evangelism*.)

There is one more important term that must be noted, and this is the Greek word *matheteuo*. This is the verb form of *mathetes* (disciple). It occurs four times in the New Testament, and will be a source of considerable interest for us in a later chapter.

Finally, we have a word on numbers. Those closest to Jesus in the Gospels are often referred to as "the Twelve," or "the twelve disciples," or "the twelve apostles". To catalogue this, there are thirty occurrences in the Gospels, one in Acts, one in 1 Corinthians and one in Revelation. In the Gospels, there are eight occurrences in Matthew, eleven in Mark, seven in Luke and four in John. When Judas Iscariot is no longer included, the Twelve becomes the Eleven, giving a further six occurrences (one in Matthew, one in Mark, and two each in Luke and Acts). For completeness, "the ten" is used twice, referring to the Twelve without James and John. (See Matthew 20:24 and Mark 10:41.) In terms of larger numbers, "the seventy-two" (or "the seventy" in some manuscripts and therefore some translations) occurs twice, in Luke 10:1 and Luke 10:17.

And with that information, we will declare that the foundation is laid!

THREE

WHO IS THE GREAT COMMISSION

FOR?

Things we regularly quote in Church meetings, whether they come from the Bible or from our developed liturgy, tend to pick up names. We can talk about the "Aaronic Blessing," the "Prayer of Humble Access," the "Golden Rule," and many, many more. The positive side of this is that names are useful and enable us to refer to whatever it is without the need of an identifying description. The downside is that we can develop an insiders' jargon that others find impossible to penetrate. Part of this jargon is the name the "Great Commission".

The term is usually said to have been coined by Dutch missionary Justinian Von Welz (1621-1668), but popularised two centuries later by the more widely known missionary Hudson Taylor. Now it has become common parlance—but perhaps not for everyone.

What is the Great Commission? One answer to that question offered in response to an online search is, "the instruction of the resurrected Jesus Christ to his disciples to spread his teachings to all the nations of the world." I would describe that as a *loose* answer, but it begins to make the point.

The more precise answer that many would tend to give would be Matthew 28:18-20, or perhaps more fully Matthew 28:16-20. That section of Scripture currently has the added paragraph heading "The Great Commission" in at least six leading English-language translations that I have consulted.

However, I have several colleagues who are missionaries and who would hold to a wider definition. They would want to include with the Matthew text the corresponding instructions from the other Gospels and the book of Acts. Here they are all together:

> [18]Then Jesus came to them and said, "All authority in heaven and on earth has been given to me. [19]Therefore go and make disciples of all nations, baptising them in the name of the Father and of the Son and of the Holy Spirit, [20]and teaching them to obey everything I have commanded you. And surely I am with you always, to the very end of the age."   Matthew 28:18-20

> [15]He said to them, "Go into all the world and preach the good news to all creation. [16]Whoever believes and is baptised will be saved, but whoever does not believe will be condemned. [17]And these signs will accompany those who believe: In my name they will drive out demons; they will speak in new tongues; [18]they will pick up snakes with their hands; and when they drink deadly poison, it will not hurt them at all; they will place their hands on sick people, and they will get well."   Mark 16:15-18

> [46]He told them, "This is what is written: The Christ will suffer and rise from the dead on the third day, [47]and repentance and forgiveness of sins will be preached in his name to all nations, beginning at Jerusalem. [48]You are witnesses of these things. [49]I am going to send you what my Father has promised; but stay in the city until you have been clothed with power from on high."   Luke 24:46-49

> [21]Again Jesus said, "Peace be with you! As the Father has sent me, I am sending you." [22]And with that he breathed on them and said, "Receive the Holy Spirit. [23]If you forgive anyone his sins, they are forgiven; if you do not forgive them, they are not forgiven."   John 20:21-23

"But you will receive power when the Holy Spirit comes on you; and you will be my witnesses in Jerusalem, and in all Judea and Samaria, and to the ends of the earth."   Acts 1:8

Perhaps, as my missionary colleagues may say, these verses constitute the Great Commission when taken together. However, having said and acknowledged that, I will from this point forward use the term Great Commission to refer to the passage from Matthew. Of course, it is the only one of the passages that uses the language of discipleship anyway.

We will deal first of all with the issue of timing raised in chapter one.

What are the last words of Jesus?

It was many years ago, before I even started pastoring. I was teaching in a high school, and once a week in the lunch break we would run a Scripture Union group, reaching out to the school students with the message of the gospel of Jesus Christ. Time was short, and one of the more effective strategies for our meeting was to show a short animated film on a story from the Bible. One particular film described the Resurrection to the Ascension. The memorable image was of Jesus on the mountain, speaking the words of the Great Commission, ending with, "... surely I am with you always to the very end of the age." Then He immediately raised His hands to bless His followers, and ascended to heaven. It was memorable, but it was wrong!

Sometimes I think that everyone I meet must have seen this film! Or at least they must have seen a film like it. There seems to be no other explanation for the persistence of the idea that the words of the Great Commission are the final words of Jesus on earth immediately prior to His Ascension. Yes, the words are the last words in Matthew's gospel, which may cause some people to think of them as the last words of Jesus, but that hardly seems to explain the persistence of the notion. Where does it come from? I have heard it dramatised in pulpits that the words of the Great Commission, being the last words of Jesus, are the marching orders for the Church. I have heard the Church compared to an army, and an army should obey its last orders until it receives new orders—but these have not yet come! Even teachers given to less drama have suggested that these last words of Jesus must be considered extra important because they *are* the last words of Jesus; and so *making disciples* must be the highest priority. With just a moment's thought we can see that this assumption cannot be true.

Jesus' Ascension is described in Acts 1:9-11. It begins, "After he said this, he was taken up before their very eyes, and a cloud hid him from their sight." What were the words He spoke immediately prior to this?

> *"But you will receive power when the Holy Spirit comes on you; and you will be my witnesses in Jerusalem, and in all Judea and Samaria, and to the ends of the earth."*   Acts 1:8

These are the last words of Jesus on earth. Yes, they are still about mission. But they are not the words of the Great Commission.

You may want to ask, "Is it not possible that Jesus *did* speak the words of Matthew 28:18-20 at this time, but they are not specifically recorded in Acts?" But the answer is no. These are *not* two different versions of the same incident. How do we know? We know because the Ascension took place on the Mount of Olives, just outside Jerusalem (see Acts 1:12). But the Great Commission took place in Galilee (see Matthew 28:16), some eighty miles to the north. These are different resurrection appearances, separated in time by at least the length of time it took for the Eleven to make the journey to Jerusalem (see Acts 1:1-4).

Who was the Great Commission given to?

Here is the whole paragraph under consideration:

> [16]*Then the eleven disciples went to Galilee, to the mountain where Jesus had told them to go.*

[17]When they saw him, they worshipped him; but some doubted. [18]Then Jesus came to them and said, "All authority in heaven and on earth has been given to me. [19]Therefore go and make disciples of all nations, baptising them in the name of the Father and of the Son and of the Holy Spirit, [20]and teaching them to obey everything I have commanded you. And surely I am with you always, to the very end of the age."

Matthew 28:16-20

Who was the Great Commission given to? Verse 16 tells us that it was given to the eleven disciples. From this we could conclude that the answer is that it was given to "disciples". Since we ourselves *are* disciples, we conclude by extension that it was given to *us*. However, Jesus made several other resurrection appearances, including one in which He appeared to "more than five hundred of the brothers at the same time" (see 1 Corinthians 15:6). Yet He did not give *them* the Great Commission. Perhaps our answer may be wrong.

Verse 16 says it was given to the eleven disciples. Let's consider the "eleven". The Eleven was the Twelve minus one, the one being Judas Iscariot. What this means is that the Great Commission was given to the *Apostles*. Further, it was not given to Peter or Andrew or James or John, but to the Apostles as a group. The plural nature of the Commission is underlined by the word "you" in verse 20 being plural in both occurrences.

Also in verse 20, we have, "teaching them to obey everything I have commanded you." This word "everything" must include the Great Commission itself. So regarding the Great Commission, we have a cyclical process, a rolling flow coming out from the Eleven. Who are these who flow out from the Eleven? It's probably safest to assume that that is the *Church*.

Who was the Great Commission given to? Summarising this argument, the answer to the question in practical terms is "the Church".

The Church — the many-membered Body of Christ

Now the Church is the Body of Christ, where there are many parts but one Body. The various parts are different each from another, serving different functions—some more visible, some more voluble, but each equally important—in *harmony* rather than in unison, in *unity* rather than in uniformity. And in that multifaceted way, the whole Body fulfils its purpose as each part does its work.

Tragically in 1982, contemporary Christian pianist, singer and songwriter Keith Green died in a plane crash. After his death, two more albums of songs were released, including "Jesus Commands Us To Go," which led to a posthumous tour conducted by co-operating missions organisations, and featuring video clips of Keith speaking and singing the songs. The words of the title track began:

> *Jesus commands us to go,*
> *But we go the other way.*
> *So he carries the burden alone,*
> *While his children are busy at play,*
> *Feeling so called to stay.*

It was emotive, powerful and challenging. But it's probably fair to say that the message was the result of understanding the Great Commission as having been given to *each* of us individually. If we are correct in concluding that the Great Commission has in reality been given to the *Church*, then we have more of a corporate response.

Bob Bishop was my overseer and my friend, and I still miss him. For many years he was President of the missions agency Globe International, then known as Globe Missionary Evangelism. In this capacity he was facilitating individuals to fulfil their callings as missionaries, in co-operation with their local church; and facilitating local churches to be involved in world missions, and to send their people and support them on the mission field. He was always looking for illustrations to help people see the importance of those who go and those who stay, and came across the axe head and the axe handle.

The axe head is the thing that does the obvious work. It cuts and slices and makes the difference. It's literally the cutting edge. On the other hand, the axe head cannot swing itself. It needs the axe handle to swing it in order than it can make its difference. If the axe head is dull or missing, then swinging the axe handle means that that which should be cut just gets clobbered. If the axe handle is broken or missing, the axe head may be sharp and shiny, but it cannot accomplish much. In the illustration, the axe head is the missionary on the front line, and the axe handle is the support system, formed from the local church and the missions agency. Both head and handle are required.

The Commission includes the command "go and make disciples of all nations". It's easiest to see that the missionaries are those who *go*, relocating to foreign cultures for the sake of love and obedience to the call. Yet they are not isolated and alone, nor are they the only ones taking the Great Commission seriously. For each visible missionary (the axe head), behind the scenes is the missions sending agency, the home church and its leaders, those giving support in prayer and encouragement, those giving financial support, and those giving relational support (the axe handle). As all these individuals fulfil their various God-given callings, in all of these areas—in the supporting and in the going—the whole church is involved in missionary endeavour.

Not all actually go. The missionaries *do* go. As the missionaries go and the others sustain, the *Church* is fulfilling the Great Commission.

FOUR

WHAT IS THE HEART OF THE GREAT COMMISSION?

The village was small and the primary school was not full term. It meant that after four years of education, I had to transfer at age nine to the primary school in the neighbouring village, one mile away. My remaining three primary school years were split between two classes, the older of which was taught by the Headmaster. That was a very different experience, because he was "old school". There was much apprehension fuelled by numerous scare stories prior to the move to *his* room. But once I got there, I loved it! There was structure and definition and clarity. It was in this class towards the top end of primary school that I had my first introduction to grammar: sentence construction; parts of speech; nouns; adjectives; verbs; adverbs; prepositions; conjunctions; participles; parsing; principal and subordinate clauses; and yet more. I loved it. It was precise, learnable, practical and useful. I noted at the time that not everyone had the same reaction to the subject—but many did. I had assumed that when I made the move to high school, we would go further, higher, and deeper into the subject. Yet it was never mentioned. We repeated a little of what I already knew, very briefly, at age 14, but only because the class requested it. I observed that many people had never heard of parsing, and were simply not taught English grammar in school. Some encountered a few of the terms in connection with studying a foreign language, but had no knowledge that "that stuff" also existed in English. I remember smiling when an acquaintance said, "German's really hard! I'm glad we don't have a subjunctive in English."

I am very grateful for my primary school education having included an introduction to grammar. It aids understanding. And I'm still drawing on it here.

The Great Commission contains four instructions:

- Go
- Make disciples of all nations
- Baptise them in the name of the Father and of the Son and of the Holy Spirit
- Teach them to obey everything I have commanded you

Written as they are above, it appears that there are four imperatives (that is, commands). However, three of them begin with a participle, making them more incidental (which does *not* mean "unimportant"). As is readily seen from the English translation, two of them are present participles, *baptising* and *teaching*. Present participles are recognised as words ending *–ing* in English. Here they indicate a continuous, ongoing action. The third participle is *go*. It is not translated *going*, as we might at first think, because this is a Greek *aorist* participle, which has no direct English equivalent. It is translated *go* in the sense of *as you go* or *when you go*, or perhaps, *having gone*. It is more of a precursor to the imperative.

The imperative is the remaining bullet point in the list above, "make disciples of all nations". The Greek word in question is *matheteuo*, the verb form of disciple (*mathetes*) that we mentioned earlier. We will take the time in a later chapter to look at the meaning and the other incidences of this word. It is translated *make disciples* in the New International Version, and in many other translations. The King James Version translates the verb as *teach*. Many people therefore conclude that the heart of the Great Commission is the imperative *make disciples*. This is a minor error with major consequences.

The consequences of the error

Some time ago in Liberty Church in Dunfermline, we were reviewing our missions policy and strategy. In this connection, we did an online search for any materials that might be helpful, and in the process came across the name of a missions consultant we did not previously know—David Mays. David lived in the Indianapolis area, and went home to be with the Lord in 2012. His published materials included some teaching on the Great Commission. It is freely acknowledged that these writings of David Mays, discovered in this accidental way, are the inspiration for the remainder of this chapter.

Let us go back to school for a few moments and remind ourselves of some basic grammar. Verbs can be transitive or intransitive. A transitive verb needs an object to complete the thought. An intransitive verb can stand alone. For example, if I say, "The dog barked," the meaning is clear. But if I say, "The dog wanted," the meaning is *not* clear. We would want to say, "The dog wanted *what?*" If instead I say, "The dog wanted a biscuit," or, "The dog wanted to go for a walk," the thought is then complete.

A stage closer to the form of words we see in the Great Commission, if I say, "Go and sleep," it is clear what I mean. But if I say, "Go and call," it's not. We would want to ask, "call *what?*" or, "call *whom?*" If instead I say, "Go and call you brother," or, "Go and call your dog," the thought is then complete.

The text of Matthew 28:19 in the King James Version says, "Go and teach all nations." We cannot say, "Go and teach." That is incomplete. We would want to ask, "teach *what?*" or, "teach *whom?*" The object is "all nations," and including the object is necessary for the sense.

But *teach* is not a good translation. The word is actually the verb form of *disciple*. If we turn the noun *disciple* into a verb, we could translate the phrase as, "Go and disciple." Again, that is incomplete and would leave us asking, "disciple *whom?*" The answer would be, "Go and disciple all nations."

However, *disciple* is not usually considered to be a proper English verb. So to maintain proper English, most of the more modern Bible versions translate the sentence as, "Go and make disciples of all nations." And here is the problem. It now seems that *make* has become the verb. It is transitive, so requires an object. "Make." Make *what?* "Make *disciples.*" And it sounds like a complete thought.

"Of all nations" is relegated to a prepositional phrase, a qualifier or modifier; but subordinate to the main thought, and easily overlooked. However, "all nations" is in fact the object. Notice that the word *of* is added for the sake of the phrase. It is not present in the Greek.

Thus the awkwardness of translation has created a distortion. People are left to assume, and many have assumed, that we are mandated in the Great Commission to *make disciples* independent of the idea of *all nations*. This has often been applied in the context of a local church, as will be discussed further in the next chapter. Clearly, it's not wrong to make disciples—no one is saying that making disciples is inappropriate! But the mandate of the Great Commission is to make disciples of all nations.

And concerning the nations ...

As an additional consideration, the word here for nations is the Greek word *ethne*, the plural of *ethnos*, and it can be used for nations, peoples, ethnic groups, or people groups. One could say that the Great Commission is more about discipling *groups* than individuals. The full phrase here is *panta ta ethne*, that is, *all the nations*. From a Jewish perspective, they would understand this as *other* nations, which is why the word *ethne* is sometimes translated as *Gentiles*. And Matthew's Gospel is certainly written from a Jewish perspective. This would make the implication that the heart of the Great Commission may in fact be, "Go and disciple nations other than yours."

Conclusion

To summarise, one little error has left so many people today thinking that the heart of the Great Commission is to "make disciples," and then they interpret this mandate primarily in the context of "our local church" and its growth. As David Mays says, the Great Commission has been domesticated. In truth, the heart of the Great Commission is: "Make disciples of all nations." And the sense of it may be: "Make disciples of all nations other than yours."

FIVE

MAKE DISCIPLES

WHO

MAKE DISCIPLES

On Saturday April 5th 1980, Mary and I were married. Clearly, it was a significant day in our lives. On the following day, we were on our honeymoon, and quite unaware of an event with its own significance that was taking place in another part of the planet. It was Easter Sunday 1980, and in Orange County, California, specifically in Laguna Hills High School Theater, there was the official launch of Saddleback Valley Community Church. There were two hundred and five people in attendance on the launch day, according to Pastor Rick Warren. Now thirty-seven years later, the attendance is well over 20,000 people, and the name Saddleback Church is known all around the world.

Having worked out his principles and methods over a period of years, Rick Warren finally went to print in 1995. The result was the book, "The Purpose-Driven Church." It proved to be massively popular, became a standard text in many Bible Colleges, and sold over one million copies worldwide. Then in 2002, he released a follow-up based on the same principles, under the title, "The Purpose-Driven Life." This was written as a 40-day devotional, and proved even more popular, breaking all the records and selling over 30 million copies by 2007.

The Purpose-Driven Church

Rick's books are based on the five purposes of the church that he sees spelled out in the New Testament. He expresses them in words and phrases in several different ways. He says that the Church should grow *warmer* through fellowship, *deeper* through discipleship, *stronger* through worship, *broader* through ministry and *larger* through evangelism. He lists the purposes as *outreach*, *worship*, *fellowship*, *discipleship* and *service*. He lists the objectives alliteratively as:

- Mission
- Magnify
- Membership
- Maturity
- Ministry

He lists the corresponding tasks, also alliteratively, as:

- Evangelize
- Exalt
- Encourage
- Edify
- Equip

He shows how these purposes emerge from the biblical text in various ways, but the major model he presents is based on two scripture passages, that he refers to as the Great Commandment and the Great Commission. The Great Commandment is understood as Matthew 22:35-40.

> [35]One of them [Pharisees], an expert in the law, tested him with this question: [36]"Teacher, which is the greatest commandment in the Law?"
>
> [37]Jesus replied: "'Love the Lord your God with all your heart and with all your soul and with all your mind.' [38]This is the first and greatest commandment. [39]And the second is like it: 'Love your neighbour as yourself.' [40]All the Law and the Prophets hang on these two commandments."

From verse 37, Rick draws the ideas of worship/magnify/exalt, and from verse 39 the ideas of service/ministry/equip. Then from the Great Commission, he adds thirdly outreach/mission/evangelize linked with the phrase, "make disciples of all nations." Fourthly he adds fellowship/membership/encourage associated with, "baptising them in the name of the Father and of the Son and of the Holy Spirit." And fifthly he adds discipleship/maturity/edify in reference to, "teaching them to obey everything I have commanded you."

He summarises the approach with a slogan that became the Saddleback motto. It has been copied, imitated and re-cycled by many others to the point of being a recognisable saying in numerous church circles. The slogan is:

> *A Great Commitment to the Great Commandment and the Great Commission will grow a Great Church.*

A present-day trend

It has become popular to use the Great Commission as part of the mission statement of a local church. Rick Warren may not have been the first pastor ever to do this. However the great popularity of his books and materials indicates that he has surely helped the trend develop. He may indeed have been a significant influence in popularising the concept that part of the mission of a local church is to fulfil the Great Commission in, through and amongst its own members, and in its own locale.

Are we to say that this concept is wrong? Many present-day pastors might consider such a concept self-evident. The question is probably best answered yes and no. "Wrong" is too strong a term, but there are two aspects of the Great Commission that simply do not fit this usage. The first of these is the phrase, "Therefore go". These words are often ignored. They seem to be redundant words in the understanding of the Commission. The implication is that others may go, but you just make disciples where you already are.

The second aspect that does not fit this usage is the phrase "of all nations". Again, it seems to be redundant language. Now it is possible to say that we have several different people-groups in the Church; but that hardly seems adequate to make the usage fit. This is of course particularly true if we are right to conclude that the correct implication of the phrase is, "make disciples of all nations other than yours".

The Great Commission in that application has therefore degenerated to, "Therefore, make disciples, baptising them in the name of the Father and of the Son and of the Holy Spirit, and teaching them to obey everything I have commanded you." This may be valid as far as it goes; but the problem is that it is *not* the Great Commission. The very heart of it has been significantly reduced.

On the other hand, it is possible to argue that when Rick Warren combines what he calls the Great Commandment and the Great Commission, he is simply *applying* them to the purposes of the church rather than saying that that is how the texts should be *interpreted*. A given scripture text will have one interpretation—it means what it means—and yet may have many *applications*. It may be argued that the Great Commission may be *applied* as Rick Warren uses it to the purposes of the church, so long as these purposes are established by other clearer texts. After all, as Rick uses it, the phrase in question—*go and make disciples of all nations*—is simply applied to *evangelism*. There is no more detailed application of the words than that. Evangelism is considered to be one of the five purposes of the church, and this phrase from the Great Commission is seen as broadly in support of that purpose.

Is there more to say?

Rick Warren applies the phrase "make disciples of all nations" to evangelism. But that is not the only possibility for those who seek to make the Great Commission the marching orders for their local church locally. There is another approach, one that is subtly different, and will require some explanation to make it clear.

Rick Warren's approach to the Great Commission is sequential. Step 1 is to "make disciples," which he sees as evangelism. Step 2 is to baptise those who are now believers as a result of the evangelism, and receive them into membership in the church. This is the phrase, "baptising them in the name of the Father and of the Son and of the Holy Spirit". Step 3 is to teach, train and equip those who have been evangelised and baptised in steps 1 and 2. This is the phrase, "teaching them to obey everything I have commanded you."

The other approach is *not* sequential. It views *making a disciple* or *discipling* as the overarching task. This task is a process and takes time. As part of this process, it sees the *baptising* phrase and the *teaching* phrase as stages within. Thus the process of *making disciples* includes *baptising* them and *teaching* them. If I am making a disciple, I will teach the person everything that I myself have been taught. When the last thing has been taught that I myself have been taught, only then will the disciple-making process be complete, and the person will then be a disciple.

Therefore the other phrases of the Great Commission are not viewed as happening subsequent to *making disciples*, as for Rick Warren; but rather are viewed as describing the whole *process* of making disciples, which includes them.

In recent years, a large number of individuals and churches have come through the influence of G12, a system of church leadership and government with a heavy emphasis on discipleship and making disciples, which emerged from Bogota, Colombia through Pastor César Castellanos. Anyone in the flow of G12 or using G12 principles will almost certainly view making disciples more akin to this second way.

Thus we have a double use of the phrase *make disciples*. To some it means evangelism, to others it describes the whole process from unbeliever to fully formed disciple. These are two very different understandings of the idea of making disciples, and both of them will talk of *making disciples who make disciples*. This one phrase will however describe two quite distinct realities.

At this point, we will simply *note* the double use of the phrase *make disciples*. We will return to it in a later chapter.

Harvest

Jesus said, *"The harvest is plentiful, but the workers are few. Ask the Lord of the harvest, therefore, to send out workers into his harvest field."* (Matthew 9:37,38)

Based on their experience of actual grain harvesting, this rings true. Harvest requires workers, and a bountiful harvest requires *more* workers. Now picture one lone worker in a ripe field that extends as far as the eye can see in every direction. The task is enormous, although the lone worker can yet do something, however minor it is when compared to the enormity of the task. But if the lone worker could train a second worker, and then each of them could train one more, then the four train another one each, and those eight repeat the process, by these four stages we have sixteen workers. The numbers increase rapidly—by the eighth stage we have 256 workers, by the twelfth stage 4,096, by the twentieth stage we have 1,048,576, and by the thirtieth 1,073,741,824. By the thirty-third stage, we would have more workers than the current population of the earth!

With the exponentially increasing numbers of workers, we can imagine reapers moving out into the limitless harvest field, reaping in all directions, and actually accomplishing the task of harvest. This is both mathematical and motivational. It is often associated with a "making disciples" approach, or more specifically a "making disciples who make disciples" approach. It fits the picture of 2 Timothy 2:2, as explored in chapter 2:

> And the things you have heard me say in the presence of many witnesses entrust to reliable men who will also be qualified to teach others.
>
> 2 Timothy 2:2

However, as noted in chapter 2, the word *disciple* is nowhere found in this text. Does this harvest picture fit with the Great Commission? We instinctively think it *should*, and we have noted several times that the Great Commission seems to describe a cyclical process. However, let's now look in more detail and see what the implications of the Great Commission actually are.

Andrew goes to Russia?

Less than an hour's drive from my house in Dunfermline in Scotland is the coastal town of St Andrews. Known to many as the home of golf, it was apparently named after Andrew, brother of Simon Peter, who in fact is the patron saint of Scotland. How did Scotland end up with a patron saint who did not ever travel to Scotland? The usual answer is that Andrew preached to the Scythians, whose descendents travelled to Scotland, and from whom many of the Scots of today may trace their ancestry. But Scotland is not the only country to claim Andrew as their patron saint. Russia claims him too, among others. For our purposes, we do not need to be concerned with all the details of the history. Let us assume for the sake of illustration that Andrew brought the Gospel to Russia by preaching to the Russians (or the ancestors of present-day Russians).

Consider Andrew and his apostolic instructions. He has gone to Russia, so the immediate task is to make disciples of the people of that nation. He sets about the task, and soon there are Russians who have begun to believe in and follow Jesus. We will call two of these Alexei and Boris. Following his instructions in the Great Commission, Andrew baptises Alexei and Boris. He then begins the process of teaching them to obey everything that Jesus commanded Andrew to do. Of course, there are many items in the catalogue, and this process takes time. It is not simply a matter of imparting information. It requires time for assimilation, adjustment, and changed behaviour. The final teaching for Andrew to pass on to Alexei and Boris is likely to be the Great Commission itself.

So Alexei and Boris are taught, "Go and make disciples of all nations (other than your own)." As a result, let us say that Alexei goes to Ukraine and Boris goes to Poland. There in these respective locations, they begin to make disciples of the people around them.

Standing back and looking at this situation, we see that the Great Commission is being faithfully obeyed. Andrew is making disciples who make disciples. However, the disciples Andrew is making are not resident in the same location as Andrew. He is in Russia, Alexei is in Ukraine, Boris is in Poland, and the disciples that they make will make disciples elsewhere again.

If Andrew is the solitary worker in the limitless harvest field referred to above, he is multiplying workers, but he is not multiplying workers in the harvest field that he himself is in. If the task for Andrew is becoming any less, it is not due to response to the Great Commission.

This is all rather counterintuitive. We would intuitively expect that making disciples who make disciples would multiply workers to such an extent that the field is harvested in every direction as if by a centrally emanating swarm of locusts! And if we are training workers who train other workers (to change the phrase to make the point), that is exactly what we would get. But if the focus is the Great Commission, followed strictly, that would *not* be the result. If our goal is to multiply workers in our locality, then in the end we would be better focusing on a text like 2 Timothy 2:2.

Some may protest that all this is overly analytical. They would say: Let's just do the Great Commission in a loose and approximate way. It's about making disciples who make disciples, and if we do that, the field will be reaped! However, if a little analysis and a few pointed questions cause the whole strategy to unravel, we must be prepared to consider that something may be wrong with our assumptions. Although it may be possible to make an *application* of the Great Commission to local church evangelism, as discussed above, it seems that the Great Commission as a strategy will always be focused on world missions, and not the local church locally.

Well, at least I'm making disciples

Pastors and church leaders are busy people, typically accustomed to doing several things at once. Some of these things are vital tasks, but some are just busy-work; some are tried and tested, and some are in the area of fads or the latest ideas. It may often be difficult to separate which is which.

Some activities and ministries are perceived to be more successful than others, and certainly less successful than expected. That can be discouraging. In the midst of discouragement and disappointment, I for one have often heard pastors and church leaders make the self-consoling comment, "Well, at least I'm making disciples." What this means is something like: "My ministry plans, programmes or activities are not going very well at the moment; but I *am* making disciples, and since that's the central focus anyway, at least I'm doing *something* that's fruitful."

There is no denying that making disciples is good, and is certainly better than *not* making disciples. However, if that is the goal with no context or qualification, how many disciples are *enough* to be making at any given time? Is it one, or two, or three, or five, or ten, or more? It's possible that we can be self-congratulatory at our present level, rest in that perceived success and miss the challenge.

On the other hand, if we take the goal from the Great Commission, it will be to make disciples *of all nations*. In that context and with that measure, we always know that no matter how much is done, there is always so much more to do. "All nations" is a big group, and it seems that the task is never finished. They are reached one at a time, no doubt; yet it remains that "making disciples of all nations" is much more challenging than simply "making disciples" in isolation.

David Mays makes the analogy with *tidying up the room I am in* as compared to *cleaning the whole house*. Either may be considered "cleaning," but there is a difference in scope and in the magnitude of the task. Tidying up the room I am in may represent valid progress towards accomplishing the greater task. But it can hardly be a justification for not accomplishing the greater task if the greater task is in fact the commission. In the same way, *making disciples* is good; yet if the task is in fact *making disciples of all nations*, the lesser task can hardly be a justification for not accomplishing the greater.

To summarise, the Great Commission is proving rather awkward to interpret and understand in the instinctive way that we think or assume it should apply. 2 Timothy 2:2 seems to encapsulate our instinct better, and yet it is not specifically about making disciples. Where do we go from here?

SIX

WHAT DOES JESUS MODEL?

My boys were both young, and at the time they shared a bedroom. Part of the bedtime routine was to encourage them to memorise suitable Bible verses, and to go over the verses previously memorised. I was the one who had to come up with suitable verses, and one of my selections was 1 John 2:6. Here it is in the New American Standard version:

The one who says he abides in Him ought himself to walk in the same manner as He walked.

This may be accurate, but it is somewhat cumbersome, and certainly would not have made the list of memory verses if we had been using the NASB!

We used the NIV, and I have always been impressed by the neat way in which the NIV renders this text:

Whoever claims to live in him must walk as Jesus did.

The verse sets the tone for Jesus modelling behaviours and responses for us to follow. There is often great challenge in this: taking His lead, following His model, patterning our lives after His example. And it is important, because whoever claims to live in Him must walk as Jesus did!

There are two ways we can come unstuck if we apply this focus too tightly. The first is that we try to imitate things unique to Jesus. For example, Jesus died on a cross for the sins of the world. As is obvious to most Christians, that fact does *not* mean that we must do it too! There were some things unique to Him in His mission. But generally we see Jesus in the gospels operating not from His Godhood, but choosing to operate as an anointed *man*, and thereby setting us the challenge of following His model.

The second way we can come unstuck is if we determine *only* to do what Jesus is recorded as doing. The assumption is that anything He did *not* do would be off limits or somehow wrong for us. We may say, "If it's good enough for Jesus, it's good enough for me." But if we make it, "If He didn't do it, then I won't either," then we will have problems with driving a car, or flying in an aeroplane, or speaking on a telephone, and a host of similar things Jesus did not do on the earth.

It remains however that His life and behaviour is a model for us. In the immediate context of foot washing, and in the wider context of serving others, He told His followers:

> *I have set you an example that you should do as I have done for you.*
>
> John 13:15

Indeed, this is sometimes considered the very heart of discipleship by which means Jesus trains His followers. John Wimber would speak of discipleship as the "show and tell" model, where the training would be in four stages:

Stage 1 – Jesus did it while they watched
Stage 2 – They did it while Jesus watched
Stage 3 – Jesus sent them to do it and check in with Him
Stage 4 – They did what they'd seen Him model

Jesus' training methods

These four stages are central to the training methods that Jesus used. There was time for instruction, more akin to a classroom model without the room. But there was also practical instruction, hands-on learning, trial and error, feedback, correction, question and answer, things *caught* as well as *taught*.

When we read through the pages of the Gospels, we are struck by the fact that Jesus did not cultivate the huge crowds and large multitudes that sometimes followed Him. He occasionally addressed the crowds to an extent, but spent much more time investing in a small group of people.

For example, in the lead-in to the passage we know as the Sermon on the Mount we have:

> Now when he saw the crowds, he went up on a mountainside and sat down. His disciples came to him, and he began to teach them, saying:
>
> Matthew 5:1,2

He left the crowds, and what may be described as a "great opportunity," in order to invest in His disciples. Jesus consistently prioritised working with His followers, especially a small group of invited followers.

When we see this, we naturally, and quite rightly, think this should be a model for us as well. Rather than seeking the multitudes for short-term benefit, we would accomplish far more of long-term and lasting significance if we were to invest ourselves in a few high-potential people and work with them consistently.

The observation is sound. This is indeed a good strategy for developing, and more specifically for developing leaders. The results may not be as visible at first, but the potential is much higher in the end.

These are Jesus' training methods, but also His model for us for how we should train. His doing these things, combined with statements like, "I have set you an example so that you should do as I have done for you," leave little doubt that the modelling in intentional.

With all these things in our minds, and often at the very forefront of our minds, it's easy to read the Great Commission also as if Jesus is saying, "I'm now sending you out to do the things that I've been doing amongst you while I've been here."

It's as if we hear Him say, "I have spent the last several years making disciples. Now I'm sending you out to make disciples, as I have modelled for you. I have set you an example that you should do as I have done for you." At first sight, it seems to make sense, because we remember that during the years of His earthly ministry, Jesus did not prioritise instruction to the crowds, but prioritised raising up the Twelve.

We have already established that Jesus *is* telling them to go and do what He's been doing in general terms. However is that really a correct understanding of the Great Commission as well? This question warrants some careful consideration.

Did Jesus obey the Great Commission?

First of all we have to admit that the question put in this way is rather false and flawed. When it comes to the Great Commission, Jesus is the Commissioner! It does not go back further than Him. In addition, He starts by saying, "All authority in heaven and on earth has been given to me. Therefore ...". Clearly no one can commission Him in that same way. Thus Jesus was not *commissioned* with the Great Commission. But let's suppose He was. Let's suppose that God the Father commissioned Jesus with these words. Did His actions in life align with this hypothetical commissioning?

Let's begin in the Farewell Discourse, where Jesus is addressing His close followers just prior to His arrest. He said:

> "I have much more to say to you, more than you can now bear. But when he, the Spirit of truth, comes, he will guide you into all truth. He will not speak on his own; he will speak only what he hears, and he will tell you what is yet to come. He will bring glory to me by taking from what is mine and making it known to you." John 16:12-14

Did Jesus tell His close followers everything He had been commanded? Apparently not, it would seem. There were things left unsaid that would later be revealed by the Holy Spirit.

Let's now consider John 4:1,2:

> The Pharisees heard that Jesus was gaining and baptising more disciples than John, although in fact it was not Jesus who baptised, but his disciples.

Did Jesus Himself baptise? It would seem not.

Now let's go to the vicinity of Tyre. Here we find Jesus interacting with a Syrophoenician woman, and He says, "I was sent only to the lost sheep of Israel." (Matthew 15:24)

Let's bring these three instances together. Jesus did not make disciples of all nations, because He was sent only to the lost sheep of Israel. He did not baptise them, because He left that work to His disciples. And He did not teach them to obey everything He had been commanded, since He left some things unsaid for the Holy Spirit to communicate later. We could fairly conclude from this that Jesus did *not* obey the Great Commission.

We started by saying that the question was flawed, so what is the value of this conclusion? The value is that it shows us that Jesus did *not* model all the behaviours that He commissioned His followers to obey in the words of the Great Commission.

However, it seems clear that Jesus did *make disciples*, and this is what we will now consider.

Who did Jesus raise up?

Jesus had many disciples. The Twelve were disciples; but so were the Seventy-Two. In chapter 6 of John's Gospel, Jesus gives a lengthy discourse on the Bread of Life. As a result, we read in John 6:60 of many of the disciples grumbling, and no longer following (verse 66). They are contrasted sharply with the Twelve (verse 67). When Jesus focuses on investing in the Twelve, we should not think of the Twelve as disciples, and as this being an investment in disciples. The Twelve *are* disciples, but that is not their defining characteristic here. Rather the Twelve are *apostles*. Jesus was developing *apostles*, who were soon to become the foundation of the Church.

This is clearly seen from the third chapter of Mark:

> *Jesus went up on a mountainside and called to him those he wanted, and they came to him. He appointed twelve—designating them apostles— that they might be with him and that he might*

> *send them out to preach and to have authority to*
> *drive out demons.*   Mark 3:13-15

Not all manuscripts have the phrase "designating them apostles," although this phrase *is* present in the parallel passage in Luke 6:13. However there is clearly a designation of the Twelve even without the phrase. They are elsewhere referred to as apostles, and later as the "apostles of the Lamb" (Revelation 21:14). Furthermore, the phrase "send them out" above is the verb *apostello*, the verb form of apostle.

Clearing the ground

This makes a major difference. Once we see that Jesus by His investment is raising up His *apostles*, the principle and the model of His training remain every bit as powerful for us in terms of developing people and developing leaders. But the modelling loses its linkage with the Great Commission. More precisely, it loses its connection with the phrase "make disciples" in the Great Commission. Suddenly, all the modelling of Jesus, as important as it is, falls away from the phrase "make disciples". With it goes the idea that *making disciples* must necessarily be a process that lasts for about three years, or for the duration of one's ministry, however it is pictured.

The ground has thus been cleared for us to be able to examine the phrase "make disciples" itself. This is what we will now do.

SEVEN

WHAT DOES IT MEAN TO

MAKE DISCIPLES?

If you have found this chapter title in the Table of Contents and turned straight to it, or if you've been flicking through the book and landed here, please stop reading the chapter at the end of this paragraph! Please go to the beginning of the book and read the argument in sequence. It is written in the order it is in for a reason, and the previous chapters are necessary for this chapter to make sense. Thank you!

The heart of the matter

If you are here, we must assume that you have read the previous chapters, and will continue on that basis.

In chapter 5, we noted that there was a double use of the phrase *make disciples*, and that we would return to it later. The phrase is used by some people to describe the beginning of a training process, and is equivalent to successful evangelism. An example of this usage, cited in the chapter, is the way the Great Commission is handled by Rick Warren. Others use the same phrase to describe the entire training process from start to finish, including the baptising and teaching stages mentioned in the rest of the Great Commission. An example of this second understanding would be G12, emerging around Pastor César Castellanos in Bogota, Colombia. These understandings cannot both be correct.

Then in chapter 4, we noted the fact that the phrase *make disciples* cannot be used in isolation. It translates a Greek verb that requires an object, and the object is "all nations".

Thus the phrase in English should be *make disciples of all nations*.

Now for the first time we will look at the verb underlying *make disciples*, and what it actually means. For this, we will return to chapter 2.

In chapter 2, we said that the Greek word translated *disciple* is the word *mathetes*. It occurs multiple times in the New Testament, though only in the Gospels and Acts, and it means "learner or pupil". The word that will now be our interest is the verb form of *mathetes*, the Greek word *matheteuo*. This verb is used both transitively and intransitively in the New Testament. When used intransitively, it means, "to be or become a learner or pupil". When used transitively, it means, "to produce a learner or pupil; to disciple, i.e. to enrol as a scholar."

The word occurs only four times in the New Testament. The first instance is in Matthew 13:52, where it is passive and intransitive, meaning, "to become a learner or pupil". The text says:

> He said to them, "Therefore every teacher of the law who has been instructed about the kingdom of heaven is like the owner of a house who brings out of his storeroom new treasures as well as old."   Matthew 13:52

The operative word is here translated *has been instructed about*. The New American Standard renders that section, "Every scribe who has become a disciple of the kingdom of heaven ...".

Secondly, in Matthew 27:57, the verb is again passive and intransitive. The text says:

> As evening approached, there came a rich man from Arimathea, named Joseph, who had himself become a disciple of Jesus.   Matthew 27:57

Joseph has become a disciple. This is consistent with the meanings above.

The third instance is Matthew 28:19, in which the verb is active and transitive. This is the Great Commission, with which we are now very familiar.

The final instance is Acts 14:21, and it is here that the major interest lies. The verb is again active and transitive, an exact parallel of its use in the Great Commission. The text says:

> They preached the good news in that city and won a large number of disciples. Then they returned to Lystra, Iconium and Antioch
>
> Acts 14:21

Translated more literally:

> After they had preached the gospel to that city and had made many disciples, they returned to Lystra and to Iconium and to Antioch
>
> Acts 14:21 NAS

This is a parallel usage to Matthew 28:19, and the making disciples described here is clearly not a long process. One could apparently preach the gospel, make disciples, and then do something else, all on the same day!

This agrees exactly with the meaning of the term when used transitively, as mentioned above, namely "to produce a learner or pupil; to disciple, i.e. to enrol as a scholar."

What we therefore find is that the phrase in the Great Commission make disciples describes an event, and not a process. It is the producing of the learner, who subsequently learns. It is the enrolment of the scholar, not his education. Thus the Bible would lead us to say that the view symbolised by Rick Warren is more accurate, and the view symbolised by G12 misses the mark. Making disciples is equivalent to successful evangelism. It does not describe the whole establishing, forming and training process.

Pull up a chair!

The implications of this discovery are far-reaching. It's at this point that we may feel most strongly that we are swimming against the tide! Pull up a chair, and have a seat for a moment. We may need to ponder this for a while, and let it sink in. It would be a mistake to dismiss it out of hand simply because it is different from the common assumptions.

Time out!

Here are some of the implications: When we say *making disciples* and have in mind the understanding of some process of establishing or forming people, shaping or moulding or training them by our modelling and example to become fully-fledged active Christian workers, we have a mismatch with the biblical position. When we model *making disciples* on Jesus taking His followers from first contact to readiness over a period of 3½ years, we have a mismatch with the biblical position. When we use the word *disciple* as a verb, tell someone, "I'll disciple you," and mean by it some process that I do to you that establishes or forms you as a true disciple, we have a mismatch with the biblical position. In each case, the result may be a good result—but it's not what *making disciples* means.

Making disciples is an event, not a process. It may be the beginning of a process, but if so, it is the *event* at the beginning. After the event, the person concerned *is* a disciple. Throughout the process, the person concerned is a disciple— he or she is not in process of *becoming* a disciple. It is worth taking time to digest these things and ponder the implications. It is easier to go with the flow, to follow the tide, because the prevailing tide is really quite strong. The truth, however, is apparently not found in that direction.

Fully disciples from the beginning

To *make disciples* is an event that results in new disciples. After that come the stages of growth and development, which may well include training and mentoring. In the Great Commission, this corresponds to "teaching them to obey everything I have commanded you." Now you may say that this clearly delineates a *process*, so what distinction is being drawn? The critical difference is that the process is *not* called "making disciples". Only the event of conversion that begins it is called "making disciples". In every case, the training is done *as* a disciple, not in order to *become* a disciple. This is a very important distinction.

As was noted in chapter 2, there are twenty-eight references to disciples in the book of Acts. All of them, with the possible exception of Acts 9:25, use the word "disciples" where we might say "believers". In fact, as we said, the New Living Translation uses the word "believers" rather than "disciples" to translate the Greek word *mathetes* almost every time it occurs. There is no sense in the New Testament of a group of fully-fledged, qualified disciples in the midst of others who are simply converts. In the New Testament, a believer *is* a disciple. He is not *becoming* a disciple or being trained to be a disciple or any such thing—he *is* a disciple from the beginning. As such, he is a *learner*. All of us, even the most senior, are always learning and growing. We never get to the place that we have "arrived".

Disciples, not just converts?

A commonly heard phrase that we noted in chapter 1 is: "Jesus calls us to make *disciples*, not just *converts*." It is easy to understand and relate to what we mean by this. Some people, once they have become believers, keenly press on down the road that we could call the pathway of discipleship—growing, learning, developing and changing. Others seem to be converts in name only—more static and sedentary, perhaps even uninterested in a discipleship journey. In some cases, it may be that such a person is not a genuine convert. However it is possible to be a genuine convert, and yet be disobedient or deficient in discipleship, or stalled and stymied in growth and development.

Yet can we say that such an unfruitful convert is not a disciple? It sounds reasonable in a practical sense. We said that the word *disciple* means *learner.* If there is no development and change, how can such a person be a learner? How then can he be a disciple? In behavioural terms, this would seem to be a description of a convert who is not a disciple. But behind the scenes, as it were, perhaps there *is* development and change, not yet visible in behavioural terms. How can we really know? Again, the New Testament knows nothing of a convert who is not a disciple. The distinction may make practical sense to us, but is it tenable?

The apostle Paul started out as Saul of Tarsus. When he was converted on the road to Damascus, his life was completely and unexpectedly changed. He had been the archenemy, and now he was one of the brothers. The disciples in Jerusalem had a hard time believing it was true. The issue was that they did not believe his conversion was genuine. Yet the way the text phrases the matter is:

> *When he came to Jerusalem, he tried to join the disciples, but they were all afraid of him, not believing that he really was a disciple.*   Acts 9:26

The question "was Paul a genuine convert?" was the same question as "was Paul really a disciple?" If he was a genuine convert, he was a disciple. If he was not a disciple, he was not a genuine convert.

We can see from this that our unfruitful genuine convert is still in fact a disciple. Even the most frustratingly unproductive genuine convert is still a disciple! So the phrase, "make disciples, not just converts" falls. Although we do see an underlying practical truth, the terms *convert* and *disciple* simply do not allow for the distinction. In reality, every believer is a disciple. Not to be a disciple is not to be saved.

Clearly we want growing, productive, fruit-bearing, self-replicating believers. The motivation to encourage and produce these growing, productive, fruit-bearing, self-replicating believers is understandable and commendable.

Let's *do* that! Let's be intentional about that process. But to call the process *making disciples* is simply to use the wrong terminology. And the terminology is important. It matters. The difference may be small, but it is very significant.

Whose disciples are they?

There are many aspects to *making disciples*. Another difference of understanding, introduced in chapter 1, concerns the question of whose disciples we are making. Some people would assume that as Jesus had His disciples who followed Him, so Peter had his disciples who followed him, and Paul had his disciples who followed him. Their approach therefore is: if I am making disciples, then I'm making my disciples who follow me. In this understanding, the phrase "make disciples" means *make your own disciples just like Jesus made* His *disciples*. In other words, the disciples you make are *your* disciples, disciples of *you*.

The alternative approach is to understand that Christian disciples are all disciples of *Jesus* and Jesus only. In this understanding, the phrase "make disciples" means *make disciples of Jesus*. The difference between these two approaches is pretty fundamental.

We said that one of the meanings of *disciple* is "one who follows another's teaching." This may cause us to ask the question, "Whose teaching am I following?" Or in other words, "To whom is my discipleship?" We hold to the teaching of Jesus. And Jesus said:

> *"If you hold to my teaching, you are really my disciples. Then you will know the truth and the truth will set you free."*   John 8:31,32

Sometimes the nature of this freedom is being able to hold to a truth that enables us to navigate the murky waters of confusion. One of my early Bible teachers, who was hugely influential in my life and ministry, was Don Loose. I can still remember a truth he taught me, and I still hear it in his voice: "Discipleship is always to Jesus." Over the years that understanding has enabled me to navigate those murky waters of confusion in this area.

It will be no surprise then that I would describe the first approach (that is, making disciples of *you*) as a very dangerous and biblically inappropriate practice. We are disciples of Jesus. *He* is the One we are learning from. When we make disciples, we make disciples of Jesus, not of ourselves.

Temporary disciples?

There is a halfway position that says, "I know they're disciples of Jesus really, but they're effectively my disciples while I'm working with them." Even this is bad language. If that is not already obvious, the correct understanding that *making disciples* describes an *event* rather than a *process* helps us see it even more clearly.

Because I imagine a process, I can easily think that a mentoring relationship is a "discipling" relationship. And then I begin to think that the people I am mentoring are *my* disciples for this season, as I am forming or training or "discipling" them. However, when I understand that making disciples is an *event*, of course I immediately know that they are Christ's disciples, not my disciples. The mentoring or apprenticing can still happen, but those concerned are always disciples of Jesus only. Paul says in 1 Corinthians 11:1, "Follow my example as I follow the example of Christ." More literally, "Be imitators of me, just as I also am of Christ." (NAS) They are following Paul's *example*, rather than following Paul's teaching. Paul wants them to follow his example as he follows Jesus, and to follow Jesus' teaching as Paul himself also does. Therefore they are disciples of Jesus, and not of Paul.

Summary

To recap, here are the main findings of this chapter. Some people understand the term *make disciples* in the Great

Commission to mean, "make converts" or "convert to Christianity" or "win as believers" or "get saved". This is the equivalent of successful evangelism, and describes a change or a happening or an event, rather than a long drawn out process. Other people understand the term to mean the whole process in which individuals are taken from zero to sufficiently trained to repeat the process themselves. This is commonly pictured as similar to Jesus raising up the Twelve over time.

Based on the meaning of the word and its usage in the New Testament, we find that the *event of successful evangelism* understanding is accurate, and not the understanding as the *process of training and developing*. The process is valid and important, but it takes place *after* the event of *making disciples*. This finding rather flies in the face of much popular teaching and assumption on the subject. The ramifications of the discovery are far-reaching, calling into question, or even contradicting, some of the teachings, assumptions and practices that are considered to be established wisdom on the matter.

What it really challenges is not so much our practices as our terminology. However, there is one important area in which it does challenge or change our practice. It is this that we will now address.

EIGHT

WHAT DIFFERENCE

DOES THIS MAKE?

The tour was called, "Let God Speak." It did the rounds of the UK in the early 1980s, including Edinburgh, where I was part of the crowd. Organised by British Youth For Christ, the evenings brought together Clive Calver, Graham Kendrick, Ishmael and others, with David Pawson as the speaker. The message made quite an impact in its day. Another of those taking part in the tour was freelance writer and poet, Steve Turner. I later saw a book of poetry by Steve Turner, and the poem that lodged in my memory was a short one called, "History Lesson". It goes like this:

> History repeats itself.
> Has to.
> No-one listens.

The message is creatively expressed, and very true. Another common expression states that we must learn the lessons of history, or else we are doomed to repeat them.

The Church is not very good at learning these lessons. Sometimes we think the lesson of history is that it "didn't work," so we respond to supposed new ideas with a rather cynical, "We tried that once before." But it is also common to find an enthusiasm amongst younger believers who are simply unaware of the history, a keenness to act on an idea, with the implicit assumption, "We are the first generation ever to think of that." This assumption is unlikely to be true! I often tell students, "We have to stay connected to what God has been doing forever."

Therefore if the general counsel is to *make disciples who make disciples*, it would be wise to consider previous discipleship movements and see what we can learn. Although an analysis of previous movements is beyond the scope of this book, we may make some general comments.

The fact that we can talk about *previous* discipleship movements indicates that something went wrong; otherwise they would still be *present* discipleship movements. They were no doubt well intentioned and well motivated, seeking to bring an appropriate response from God's people to God, His word and His will, resulting in increased holiness or accountability or fruitfulness or growth and multiplication. Yet for many they ended up in an unhealthy and unhelpful place, with accusations and evidences of manipulation, legalism and control. Seeking to understand and interpret the operative biblical texts as accurately as possible must be an important factor in staying on track—and it is the best hope of not repeating past errors. So what difference does this study make?

Clones and copies

Instead of being a person, if I were information on a sheet of paper, I could be scanned and printed several times, resulting in instant multiplication! Of course, people are more complex; although multiplying disciples by cloning is the equivalent thought. The goal of some Christian workers is to reproduce themselves in ministry, at least once and perhaps multiple times. The thinking is: *unless I reproduce myself in ministry, I will eventually die out*. It is not normal to put this into words, but if we could capture the script behind the intention, it might read something like this:

> *I am called of God and commissioned to do what I do. I know that I am not perfect, but I also know that I am valid, useful and effective in ministry. I desire to reproduce myself to increase the number of effective workers like me, or at least ensure continuance in this ministry after me.*

Usually people working from that unspoken script would protest, "I'm not looking to make an exact copy of *me*. I'm looking to prepare someone who can take forward the kinds of things I've been doing in his or her own way."

There is nothing wrong with that of course — unless it gets tangled up with the thoughts and language of making disciples. Then we have a problem.

If making disciples means *raising up people like me*, then we are certainly thinking of a *process* and not an *event*, and we are certainly thinking of disciples of *me* rather than of Jesus. For two reasons therefore the language of making disciples is not appropriate.

Again for the sake of clarity, there is nothing wrong with the desire to reproduce oneself in ministry. But we must not call it *making disciples*. To do so would simply not be a biblical fit; and it would distort and obscure all that we have discovered about discipleship in truth.

My discipleship

As we said in the previous chapter, to *make disciples* is an event that results in new disciples. At the moment that I become a disciple, my discipleship begins. (This may sound self-evident, but we have to be clear.) My discipleship then continues and does not end this side of glory.

My discipleship is not something that is being done *to me*. Discipleship is not another word for what some would call "discipling". My discipleship is the process of my following Jesus. I live my life as a believer in Jesus. That is my discipleship. A disciple is a *follower* of Jesus, and the following continues. A disciple is a *learner*, and the learning does not stop. There is no point of graduation where my discipleship ends. My life as a disciple of Jesus is my discipleship. It continues for as long as my life on earth does.

Along the path of my journey of discipleship, I can be helped, or I can be trained, or I can be mentored for a season. This is all good language. Yet throughout it all my discipleship continues, because I continue to be a disciple of Jesus.

No "process period"

Because my discipleship continues, there is no "process period" of three weeks or six months or three years during which I am being "discipled". My discipleship begins the moment I become a believer, and I walk it out every day of my Christian life. There is no graduation to fully-fledged disciple. Discipleship is continuous.

Making disciples is not a process that somebody takes me through, and it is not a process that I do to a new believer. Therefore there is no process period. The emphasis is off the *processing* of new believers. That is not to say that new believers do not need help. They may well need help, and are highly likely to benefit from it. But the emphasis is on *help*, not *treatment*.

Many have turned what they have termed *discipling* into something akin to a rite of passage, in which I do to a new believer what he cannot do for himself, as a result of which and at the end of which he becomes established as a disciple in his own right. During the process, he has to endure and keep going because he is not yet "discipled". The treatment is not yet complete. Once the treatment *is* complete, and he has been "discipled," then he gets his independence back. He is considered a disciple now, and is ready to repeat the process by becoming a "discipler" of another new believer.

It is not the *cycle* that is problematic here. It is *good* to help others as you have been helped; it is *good* to pass on to new believers what you have learned, perhaps because others passed it on to you. What is problematic is the rite of passage aspect, where you are given *treatment* by being taken through a necessary process called "discipling," without which you will probably not be "ready".

That is not to say that there are always problems. But by using the language of *making disciples* to describe the process of establishing new believers, there is always the *potential* for problems.   Again, *helping* is positive and beneficial, rather than *treatment*.   There is room in helping for befriending, for coaching, and for mentoring.   Rather than exercising superiority, this is more of a functional assistance.   But the language of *making disciples* when used here is inappropriate terminology.

Legalism and control

Particularly in the West, God's people have a tendency to be very individualistic.   We are often fiercely independent, generally considering it a good thing.   This attitude has many positive consequences, and also some negatives.   One of the negative consequences is an instinctive reaction against leadership and authority.   We often feel, and sometimes express, "You can't tell me what to do!"   Now there are positive aspects even to this reaction, and yet it often leads to bad behaviour.

Observing this, some leaders have honestly tried to help to regulate the behaviour.   Though done with the best of intentions, it has sometimes gone too far.   To put it in the terms we have been using, the "process period" becomes indefinite, and the person is effectively considered as some kind of "permanent disciple".   The word "disciple" may not be emphasised.   Other language brought to bear might be: "You are one of my twelve"; or, "You are on my permanent team."   Or perhaps there is a change of metaphor, and it becomes, "I am your Shepherd."   The problem comes not with the terms *per se*, but with the overemphasis on the regulation of behaviour.

The lady was a medical doctor and a Christian.   She was invited to join an advisory group of a small local charity broadly in her field.   Her reaction was, "I'd like to, but I'll have to check with my cell group leader."   Now, it is one thing to seek *advice*—advice can be helpful.   But it is another thing entirely to have to seek *permission*; and that seemed to be the issue here.   If the cell leader did not think it right for her, she would not do it, whatever she herself thought.

For a given possibility, there are two sides to this. One side is: I think the possibility is OK, but if my leader/shepherd does not think it is right for me, I will not do it. The other side is: my leader/shepherd thinks this possibility is right for me, therefore I will do it, even though I myself do not have any desire to do it or any sense that it is right. I do it or do not do it not for reasons of my primary decision, but for reasons of secondary control.

I have primary responsibility for the decisions in my life that are mine to make.   Other people may have *secondary* responsibility for some of these decisions.   But secondary responsibility is always secondary. The problem comes when I allow my leader/shepherd, who may have a *secondary* responsibility, to be determinative in the decision, and think of it as obedience to or compliance with the will of God. That effectively hands him *primary* responsibility in the area of *my* personal responsibility, and results in control.

Legalism is a widely used word. We can overuse it, and we are capable of using it as a self-defensive exclamation when we do not want to do something! Consider the following.

A man takes a dog on a lead, walking through the busy streets of the town. He is concerned for the safety of the dog, not wanting it to run off and be lost, and not wanting it to stray into traffic and be knocked down by a bus. However, some passers-by make their opinions known that it is cruel to treat the dog so restrictively by holding it on a lead, and tell him that he should give the dog its liberty by freeing it from the tether. Perhaps he does, unclipping the lead from the dog's collar, and the dog runs off and is never seen again, or immediately walks into the roadway and is knocked down by a bus, just as he had feared. The motivation for keeping the dog on the lead is perhaps partly control, but is also for the safety, protection and wellbeing of the dog.

The dog on the lead is a picture of legalism, walking under rules. The dog may not be free, but it is safe. And it does not have much thinking to do. It is easy for the dog to walk on the lead. When the man unclips the lead from the collar, the dog is walking unrestrained. It could intentionally run away, it could run off and get lost, or its new-found freedom could result in its danger or demise on the road. If walking on the lead is a picture of legalism, then this is a picture of licence, walking unrestrained.

However, there is a third way. This is not some tepid middle-of-the-road compromise between legalism and licence, but a genuine third way. It is not appropriate for the puppy that does not know any better. But once the dog reaches a certain stage, the man can slip off the lead, and give the command, "Heel." The dog is untethered, free to run away, or free to wander into the busy road. But it doesn't. It chooses to obey the master's voice and walk in step with the master. Constraint there is, but the constraint is internal, not external. It requires more thinking on the dog's part, and it is more risky. Yet there are other benefits. There is more responsibility being exercised, with evidence of maturity and obedience.

In a general application to New Testament believers, we walk neither under rules in legalism, nor unrestrained in licence, but we walk in the Spirit. It is always possible for us to run away and do our own thing, or to run into traffic to our danger and pain. However, we choose by an *internal* constraint to obey the Master, and walk in step with Him, following the Master's voice.

In those terms, we can see a principle concerning the location of control: whenever the control on your behaviour is external to *you*, that is legalism. Walking in the Spirit is following an *internal* constraint.

Returning to the leader/shepherd discussion, having received input from your leader/shepherd, *you* may decide to do or not to do something or other. That is an internal constraint in operation. However, if in seeking to do the will of God, you do or do not do that thing simply and solely because of what your leader/shepherd says, the control on your behaviour is external to you; and that is legalism.

Discipleship (or specifically what some would refer to as "discipling"), when pictured as processing other people, is closely associated in its outworking with legalism and control.

Yet if we can learn the lessons of these earlier chapters and at the same time capture the *principles* of what we are attempting to do, legalism and control are far less likely, and certainly not inevitable. The difference is quite marked.

Why won't you stay in your place?

I have seen it happen a number of times, and possibly so have you. One such occasion immediately comes to mind. Maggie (not her real name) had become a Christian and joined the local church. She was zealous and keen, and excited to pass on her new faith to all the people she met. John and Sharon (again, not their real names), a couple in the Church, had been Christians for many years. They befriended Maggie and began to mentor and help her. This meant that they, and particularly Sharon, would regularly meet with Maggie, share and discuss things, pray, and so on. All this was good, and Maggie appreciated it. However, Sharon viewed this as a "discipling" relationship, and would have said that she was "discipling" Maggie. The problem in this arrangement was that Maggie grew rather quickly as a Christian, to the point that she was matching or exceeding Sharon in terms of spiritual growth and maturity. What happens now?

Picture it this way. As believers, we are all following Jesus. However, Sharon has her back to Jesus, as it were, looking back to Maggie, who is further back than her, further away from Jesus. Sharon is focused on *processing* Maggie. Presumably Sharon is following Jesus by walking backwards. But Maggie is growing quickly, and closing in on Sharon. Does this push Sharon closer to Jesus, provoking her and making her run backwards more quickly? Perhaps. But what usually happens is that Sharon pushes back on Maggie, and keeps her further back, so that she does not violate the "discipling relationship". What Sharon is feeling and sometimes even saying, is, "I'm discipling you. You can't run ahead of me!" In other words, "Why won't you stay in your place?" And so Maggie can be controlled, suppressed and stunted in her growth because of Sharon's "discipleship" of her.

What *should* happen? What does the Bible say?

Follow my example, as I follow the example of Christ.   1 Corinthians 11:1 (NIV)

Be imitators of me, just as I also am of Christ.
                1 Corinthians 11:1 (NAS)

What should happen?   Sharon should turn around, face forward and follow Christ. Maggie, who is behind her, can then follow her example as *she* follows Christ. And if Maggie is growing faster than Sharon, she can catch her up and run right past her.   She is then no longer following Sharon's example, but she is still following Christ; and others will be following Maggie. There is no suppression, no control, and no restriction. Mentoring can take place meaningfully and in a self-regulating way. We are automatically not mentored by someone who is behind us! And we are all moving forward following Christ.

Alternatively, if we are being processed towards graduation as a "disciple," or if we are in the business of personally processing others, thinking that in so doing we are *making disciples*, then we are in a kind of discipleship system that the Church has been in before. And the seeds of legalism and control are already well sown. It's only a matter of time.

Summary

My discipleship is my following Jesus, my living life as a follower of Jesus. It is about life-long learning. But of course it is also about obeying Jesus, implementing the things I have learned.

Making disciples is really about successful evangelism. *Making disciples* is not about producing clones or successors. *Making disciples* is not a period of you processing a new believer so that he becomes established and turned into someone like you who can then repeat that process with other new believers. (That may have merit, but it is not *making disciples* in a biblical sense.)   *Making disciples* is not about exercising control over another person's life to help him stay safe and make the right decisions; nor is it about you allowing a leader or shepherd to make the right decisions for *you*. *Making disciples* does not involve restricting or suppressing others, keeping them in their place under you as you "disciple" them. Being mentored may involve imitating or following the example of others as they follow Christ.   But mentoring is done while facing forward, following Jesus.   That change of emphasis releases bottlenecks and blockages to growth and development, and significantly helps in reducing the dangers of legalism and control.

Having done the study in the earlier chapters, this chapter asks the question, "What difference does this make?"   My hope is that we may be able to identify the helpful principle and set it free from the restrictions of wrong terminology. And at the same time, understand correctly the language of discipleship and the meaning of the instruction to *make disciples of all nations*.

However my biggest hope for this approach is that we may experience the dynamic of discipleship, and all the benefits of mentoring, without the negatives of legalism and control.

NINE

WHERE DO WE GO FROM HERE?

Cooking programmes are popular television these days. TV chefs or competitions to find budding new chefs capture our imagination and hold our interest. It is often fascinating to see how dishes on the menu are constructed. On the other hand, one of the popular ideas is to serve some dishes *deconstructed*. Perhaps there is a deconstructed cheesecake, or a deconstructed apple crumble. At first interesting, it can quickly become frustrating. The *constructed* versions are generally more popular to eat!

Something similar can happen with certain kinds of Bible teaching. Concepts and strategies that are generally accepted as established truth may be reviewed, and some aspects called into question, or even challenged. The result is akin to deconstructing the concept or strategy, and leaving the various disassembled pieces on the table. It may be interesting, but they do not have practical usefulness in that condition. The question is: can they ever be put back together again? And if so, will they work?

Most of us are practical in our focus and are motivated to help and to serve, and to get the job done. All this deconstruction seems to be an exercise in speculative delay, and that can be frustrating in itself. At the same time, we realise that our concepts and strategies are not above the possibility of being wrong, at least in part. They may have been constructed in error or by making incorrect assumptions. We also realise that some of our practices do not actually work very well. Perhaps a review might therefore improve our effectiveness. So we go along with the review, even with interest. Yet more frustration lies ahead.

We try to talk about the ministry we are involved with, but then realise that that particular phrase cannot be used now because it was found to be wrong in some way in the review. So we search for an alternative, but we do not find one. We simply do not have alternative language. This is frustrating! Perhaps we try again, because the points made by the review were interesting and did sound right. However after a short while we can be so frustrated that we do one of two things. Either we reject all the findings of the review and try to continue as before; or in the light of the review, we change our practice, which generally means that we suspend our practice.

This is the danger of deconstruction. It can take away our language, and leave us neutralised.

In the preceding chapters, we have deconstructed the Great Commission in Matthew, and especially the concept of *making disciples*. We have found that making disciples is tantamount to successful evangelism. We have found that the phrase "make disciples" describes an event and not a process. We have found that the verb *disciple* as it is commonly used is incorrect. We have found that *make disciples* cannot be separated from *of all nations*, and cannot be used independently without changing the meaning. In that way, the Great Commission in Matthew is a *world missions* text. A local church can employ the Great Commission to describe its work to the ends of the earth, but not to describe its work or inform its mission in its own locality.

These findings frustrate us because they are challenging concepts and practices we thought we knew and have focused on for years. If the findings are true, we do not know how to talk about it any more because everything is different. As a result, either we back off; or we reject the findings in the book and try to continue as if we had never read it! Yet *both* of these outcomes would be a wrong response.

Again, this is the danger of deconstruction. It can take away our language, and leave us neutralised.

If the findings of the preceding chapters are valid, then we have to attempt some kind of reconstruction. We have to put it back together again in a serviceable way. It may be different — but it should work.

Attempting a reconstruction

There is great hope here in a fact that we have also noted in a previous chapter: The Apostle Paul did not use the language of discipleship. The word *disciple* never occurs in his letters. Nor does it occur in the other letters. In fact, as we noted in chapter 2, the word *disciple* in the New Testament occurs only in the Gospels, and in Acts up to and including chapter 21. Perhaps then some suitable alternative language can be found in Paul's Letters or the General Letters.

The first thing to do is to try to identify the important principles that we have been trying to express in the language of *making disciples* in the Great Commission. What are the aspects that are vital to our concept and vision?

There are many things we could say, but my suggestion would be that there are two main principles, namely:

- Multiplying workers, and
- Producing *active* believers

Using "discipleship" language, we would call these:

- Making disciples who make disciples, and
- Making disciples, not just converts

If we are not using the word "disciples," then we need another word. A helpful clue might come from Jesus in Matthew chapter 9 and in Luke chapter 10:

> *"The harvest is plentiful, but the workers are few. Ask the Lord of the harvest, therefore, to send out workers into his harvest field."*
> Matthew 9:37,38; Luke 10:2

The word for "send out" here is not the word used for sending the Twelve or the Seventy-two. It means, "thrust forth". (The word is *ekballo*, which would literally mean, "throw out".) There is therefore a forceful sense to the sending. But the major point is that the need is for *workers*, and those sent out are *workers*.

Add to this the observation that Paul frequently speaks of his fellow *workers* (at least eleven times). Perhaps therefore

"Christian workers" would be a good alternative to "disciples" for our purposes here.

A "worker" clearly *works*. In other words, he or she is a contributor; a giver, rather than someone who only receives. The idea is automatically of someone who is *active*, rather than a passive pew-filler. However a willingness to *give* rather than only to take may not always result in a valuable contribution. He or she may do work, but not do *good* work. In order to be effective or fruitful, it is likely that the new worker will need some basic training. This training may take the form of one-to-one coaching, helping a new convert become established. Yet we must make allowance for the possibility that the training could be the direct ministry of the Holy Spirit, as a zealous new convert reads his Bible, prays and obeys, with no human agent involved.

There is a minor danger in using this term that it might be misunderstood by being confused with salvation by works. It should be clear that a Christian worker is someone who is active rather than passive as a believer. What should *not* be thought is that the person works in any sense as a condition of salvation, or even in order to earn God's favour or approval. Favour and approval are already established. We are justified by faith and stand in grace, saved "not by works, so that no one can boast." (See Romans 5:1,2 and Ephesians 2:8,9.)

There is a picture of *serving* here. As in the parable in Luke 17:7-10, there is no sense of working in order to win favour. Rather, the serving attitude is:

> "We are unworthy servants; we have only done our duty." Luke 17:10

New Christian workers may come from new believers as considered above. It is also possible that new workers may come from existing Christians, even longstanding Christians, who in the past have been more passive. They may even have been classical pew-fillers, but have now caught a spark and come to new active life! In practical terms, this may be less likely, but the possibility always exists and should never be excluded.

How do we see increased numbers of Christian workers? First of all, we should pray for it. We have already quoted this text:

> "The harvest is plentiful, but the workers are few.
> Ask the Lord of the harvest, therefore, to send out
> workers into his harvest field."
>
> Matthew 9:37,38; Luke 10:2

According to this text, sending out workers is something the Lord does. But we can *ask*. (The underlying word is stronger than "ask" sounds to us—an alternative would be "beseech".)

Having said that, the main way we see increased numbers of Christian workers is by evangelism and gathering new believers (the "make disciples" event that we talked about), and then raising them up by a process that may include befriending, training, coaching, and mentoring, separately or in combination. In the case of existing believers, we may need some breakthrough of vision or inspiration, which may come through preaching, and thereafter the same befriending, training, coaching or mentoring.

The term "Christian worker" however is clear, and it lends itself to the language of recruitment and personal challenge.

An old friend

We have mentioned the verse 2 Timothy 2:2 several times already, to the point that it has almost become an old friend. Here it is again in two versions:

> And the things you have heard me say in the
> presence of many witnesses entrust to reliable
> men who will also be qualified to teach others.
>
> 2 Timothy 2:2 NIV

> The things which you have heard from me in the
> presence of many witnesses, entrust these to
> faithful men who will be able to teach others also.
>
> 2 Timothy 2:2 NAS

In both of these translations, the object of the trust is *men*, so first of all we must note that the underlying word is a generic term that can refer to men or women. In the one translation, the men (that is, *people*) are described as *reliable*, and in the other as *faithful*—an apparent difference, and yet not a particularly significant one in that the two words are closely related in their meanings.

A second apparent difference between the translations that deserves a comment is the idea that the people given the trust are *qualified* in the one case and *able* in the other. The underlying word here carries the sense of sufficient, adequate and competent. Stringing these words together, the people these things are entrusted to should be *qualified, able, sufficient, adequate* or *competent* to teach others.

In reviewing translations and considering some of the words, this verse would seem to be a very suitable basis for the idea of multiplication, specifically of multiplying workers; or, in "discipleship" language, making disciples who make disciples. This verse could indeed be the alternative to the Great Commission that we are looking for.

Review

At this point, it would be useful to look again at what it is that we are considering here and what the issues are. The Great Commission is a very important text, and we are certainly not trying to ignore it or undermine it in any way. However, we have noted that it is really a motivation to world missions, and not a basis for what a local church should do in its own local area. This presents a problem, because we hold some cherished principles, particularly principles of establishing active workers and of the multiplication of workers; principles that we think are correct, yet we have expressed them in biblical language that has emerged from the Great Commission. If that has now been called into question as a basis for these principles locally, are the principles in fact sound? If we can see that the same principles emerge from other texts, giving an alternative basis, then we can be freshly confident that the principles are indeed sound. However we may have to express them in different biblical language.

2 Timothy 2:2 seems to be a clear basis both for investing ourselves in others who will in turn similarly invest themselves; and for multiplication and expansion as that process is continued with more and more people.

Considering the implications

Paul was writing to Timothy, and Timothy was the one taking action in response. The action called for was to entrust certain things to certain people. This was what Timothy was called to do, and what we are called to do in the application. But before we consider *doing* anything, let us consider the context. In the previous verse, Timothy was encouraged to "be strong in the grace that is in Christ Jesus." Before he was called on to *do*, he was called on to *be*. This is appropriate for us also. Everything we do in regards to establishing and multiplying workers should be done out of the strength of grace in Christ Jesus.

Having settled that, we consider the things we have heard him say "in the presence of many witnesses." The witnesses may be considered to give testimony to the *fact* that we were instructed, and also to give testimony to the *content* of that instruction. Either way, this is not some private knowledge, secretively shared, and to be passed on with equal secrecy and great selectivity. No, this is open information, shared in the presence of many, and yet its faithful passing on is important.

The things we are to pass on are the things we ourselves have been taught. This takes the pressure off. It does not *preclude* adding some other things that we may have learned by experience, but equally it does not require it. Additionally, it is healthy and helpful to pass on what we know. In one sense, something we have been told or instructed in has not really been learned or become part of us until we have passed it on to someone. Passing it on can be like pressing the "enter" key so that it actually "goes in." It can also be a way of growing and increasing ourselves. The principle of Luke 6:38 applies, "Give, and it will be given to you."

The people you entrust these things to are to be faithful or reliable people who are qualified to teach others. Yet you are not responsible for those "others". You are responsible only for passing on what you have received, which again takes the pressure off. You will want to pass it on to the right people, to faithful or reliable people. This is perhaps analogous to not throwing your pearls to pigs (see Matthew 7:6). Yet it remains that your responsibility ends with passing on the trust. Who the "others" are need not be your concern. Remember that for the people you entrust these things to, those who to *you* are the "others," to *them* are their "faithful people".

One of the things that Timothy had heard from Paul was of course 2 Timothy 2:2. In other words, when it comes to the command to pass on the things he had heard from Paul to faithful people who will be able to teach others, that command itself was to be passed on. This gives an ongoing, rolling cyclical feel to the command, as we discovered for the Great Commission. If anything, the cyclical process is even clearer, since there is no "go" stage to disrupt the geographical continuity. What results is the pure multiplication of workers.

We have already played with the numbers in chapter 5. There we pictured one lone worker in a harvest field. And we said if the lone worker could train a second worker, and then each of them could train one more, then the four train another one each, and those eight repeat the process, by these four stages we would have sixteen workers. By the eighth stage we would have 256 workers, by the twelfth stage 4,096, by the twentieth stage we would have 1,048,576, and by the thirtieth 1,073,741,824. By the thirty-third stage, we would have more workers than the current population of the earth! Therefore if each stage took six months to a year, we would have more workers than people worldwide in somewhere between seventeen and thirty-three years!

Let us now return to the image in chapter 5 of the lone worker in the middle of a ripe harvest field that stretches as far as the eye can see in all directions. As a solitary reaper, he or she would appear to make little impact. But if we can see the exponentially increasing numbers of workers in accordance with 2 Timothy 2:2, we can imagine reapers moving out into the limitless harvest field, reaping in all directions, and actually accomplishing the task of harvest.

Changing the language

Regarding the multiplication of workers and the idea of getting the job done, 2 Timothy 2:2 is not only a good basis for the Church, but I submit that it is actually a clearer and more effective basis than the Great Commission, in this regard.

What of the implications for the language that we use to describe the process on this basis? On the old basis we would talk of *making disciples*, and therefore talk of multiplication as *making disciples who make disciples*. When we combine Luke 10:2 with 2 Timothy 2:2, and note that the process is akin to reproduction, perhaps the language might be *raising up 0workers*. Multiplication could then be stated as *raising up workers who raise up workers*.

This may seem to be a shallow conclusion of a purely semantic nature. However it is my earnest hope that the idea can maintain all the positive aspects of the old basis, whilst eliminating the negative.

And so ...

We have been on a long journey of swimming against the tide. The prevailing tide sees the task in terms of making disciples who make disciples. The idea is good, but there is a major problem and confusion with the understanding of *making disciples*. This is at the heart of a more general problem with the Great Commission in an attempt to apply it to the work of a local church in its local area. Although the problem is more one of terminology than principle, the difference is critically important.   If not addressed, it has resulted, does result, and probably will always result in unnecessary legalism and control.   There is however an alternative.   Noting that the language of discipleship is found only in the Gospels, and in the book of Acts as a collective term for believers, it is possible to recast the principles of growth, development and progress on a different New Testament basis from the language of discipleship.   Doing so has no negative impact on progress, and will hopefully avoid the unnecessary legalism and control.

> *And the things you have heard me say in the presence of many witnesses entrust to reliable men who will also be qualified to teach others.*
>
> 2 Timothy 2:2

Let us go forward in a fiery and faithful way, multiplying workers, or *raising up workers who raise up workers*.   Let us keep in mind the actual last words of Jesus on the earth:

> *"But you will receive power when the Holy Spirit comes on you; and you will be my witnesses in Jerusalem, and in all Judea and Samaria, and to the ends of the earth."*   Acts 1:8

Let us truly make disciples of all nations, baptising them in the name of the Father and of the Son and of the Holy Spirit, and teaching them to obey everything we ourselves have been commanded.

Finishing Matthew 28:20, we give Jesus the last word:

> *"And surely I am with you always, to the very end of the age."*

APPENDIX

A LIST OF THE WORDS INVOLVED

Occurrences of the word *mathetes* (disciple) in NA27

Matthew
5:1
8:21
8:23
9:10
9:11
9:14 *
9:14
9:19
9:37
10:1
10:24
10:25
10:42
11:1
11:2 *
12:1
12:2
12:49
13:10
13:36
14:12 *
14:15
14:19
14:19
14:22
14:26
15:2
15:12
15:23
15:32
15:33

15:36
15:36
16:5
16:13
16:20
16:21
16:24
17:6
17:10
17:13
17:16
17:19
18:1
19:10
19:13
19:23
19:25
20:17
21:1
21:6
21:20
22:16 †
23:1
24:1
24:3
26:1
26:8
26:17
26:18
26:19
26:26
26:35

26:36
26:40
26:45
26:56
27:64
28:7
28:8
28:13
28:16

Mark
2:15
2:16
2:18 *
2:18 *
2:18 †
2:18
2:23
3:7
3:9
4:34
5:31
6:1
6:29
6:35
6:41
6:45
7:2
7:5
7:17
8:1
8:4

Mark
8:6
8:10
8:27
8:27
8:33
8:34
9:14
9:18
9:28
9:31
10:10
10:13
10:23
10:24
10:46
11:1
11:14
12:43
13:1
14:12
14:13
14:14
14:16
14:32
16:7

Luke
5:30
5:33   *
6:1
6:13
6:17
6:20
6:40
7:11
7:18   *

7:18   *
8:9
8:22
9:14
9:16
9:18
9:40
9:43
9:54
10:23
11:1
11:1   *
12:1
12:22
14:26
14:27
14:33
16:1
17:1
17:22
18:15
19:29
19:37
19:39
20:45
22:11
22:39
22:45

John
1:35   *
1:37   *
2:2
2:11
2:12
2:17
2:22

3:22
3:25   *
4:1
4:2
4:8
4:27
4:31
4:33
6:3
6:8
6:12
6:16
6:22
6:22
6:24
6:60
6:61
6:66
7:3
8:31
9:2
9:27
9:28
9:28   ‡
11:7
11:8
11:12
11:54
12:4
12:16
13:5
13:22
13:23
13:35
15:8
16:17
16:29

John	20:25	9:26
18:1	20:26	9:26
18:1	20:30	9:38
18:2	21:1	11:26
18:15	21:2	11:29
18:15	21:4	13:52
18:16	21:7	14:20
18:17	21:8	14:22
18:19	21:12	14:28
18:25	21:14	15:10
19:26	21:20	16:1
19:27	21:23	18:23
19:27	21:24	18:27
19:38		19:1
20:2	Acts	19:9
20:3	6:1	19:30
20:4	6:2	20:1
20:8	6:7	20:30
20:10	9:1	21:4
20:18	9:10	21:16
20:19	9:19	21:16
20:20	9:25 ?	

*	Disciples of John the Baptist
†	Disciples of the Pharisees
‡	Disciples of Moses
?	Unclear whether they are disciples of Paul or Jesus

All other references above are disciples of Jesus

Occurrences of the other words

mathetria (female disciple)   *summathetes* (fellow disciple)

Acts 9:36   John 11:16

matheteuo – the verb form of *mathetes* (disciple)

Matthew 13:52   Matthew 28:19
Matthew 27:57   Acts 14:21

Also by George Alexander

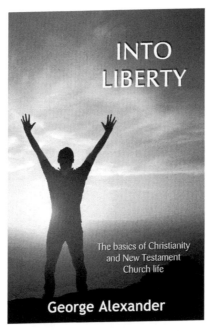

ISBN 978-0-9955601-0-9

Just to the north of Edinburgh lies Dunfermline, an ancient capital of Scotland, famous both for its Abbey and as the birthplace of Andrew Carnegie. In more recent times, Dunfermline has been the centre of operations for Liberty Church, which has flourished there since its formation in 1979.

This book has emerged from amongst the people of that Church. It began its life as the membership course for those considering joining Liberty Church. *Into Liberty* contains a blending of the basics of Christianity with practical biblical principles for living as part of a Church community, written in a direct and straightforward style. The result is a powerful primer on the Christian life. Every believer in Jesus will benefit from reading it.

There follows a sample chapter from the book:

SAMPLE CHAPTER

POWER FROM ON HIGH

KEY VERSE: I am going to send you what my father has promised; but stay in the city until you have been clothed with power from on high.   Luke 24:49

The last recorded words of Jesus on earth are found in Acts 1:8. He said: *"...But you will receive power when the Holy Spirit comes on you; and you will be my witnesses in Jerusalem, and in all Judea and Samaria, and to the ends of the earth."*

Sometimes we talk about propositional truth. Well, what we have here is *prepositional* truth! Speaking of the Holy Spirit, Jesus predicted "another Counsellor to be with you forever" (John 14:16). Notice the preposition "with". He then said that the Holy Spirit "lives with you and will be in you." (See John 14:17.) We could say that at the time of speaking He lives *with* you, and at a time future to that He will be *in* you. Clearly, we can see for example in Romans 8:11 that the Holy Spirit lives *in* us. But then in Acts 1:8, Jesus speaks about the Holy Spirit coming *on* or *upon* us, a different preposition again. Selwyn Hughes used to teach, "The Holy Spirit is *with* us to *convict*, *in* us to *convert*, and *upon* us to *clothe* [i.e. empower]." It clearly seems to be the case that references to the Holy Spirit *upon* are consistently linked with the *power* of the Spirit. We'll keep that in mind as we examine the Scriptures, looking at four relevant passages.

First of all, Pentecost:

> *[1]When the day of Pentecost came, they were all together in one place. [2]Suddenly a sound like the blowing of a violent wind came from heaven and*

filled the whole house where they were sitting.
³They saw what seemed to be tongues of fire that
separated and came to rest on each of them. ⁴All
of them were filled with the Holy Spirit and began
to speak in other tongues as the Spirit enabled
them.

⁵Now there were staying in Jerusalem God-
fearing Jews from every nation under heaven.
⁶When they heard this sound, a crowd came
together in bewilderment, because each one heard
them speaking in his own language. ⁷Utterly
amazed, they asked: "Are not all these men who
are speaking Galileans? ⁸Then how is it that each
of us hears them in his own native language?
⁹Parthians, Medes and Elamites; residents of
Mesopotamia, Judea and Cappadocia, Pontus and
Asia, ¹⁰Phrygia and Pamphylia, Egypt and the parts
of Libya near Cyrene; visitors from Rome ¹¹(both
Jews and converts to Judaism); Cretans and Arabs
— we hear them declaring the wonders of God in
our own tongues!" ¹²Amazed and perplexed, they
asked one another, "What does this mean?"
¹³Some, however, made fun of them and said,
"They have had too much wine."   Acts 2:1-13

Notice that in verse 3, the tongues of fire came to rest *upon*
them. In verse 4, the language is of being "filled with the
Spirit", and yet Pentecost is clearly presented as the fulfilment
of Acts 1:8, when the Holy Spirit would come *upon* them.
Clearly too they spoke in tongues. On the basis of verses 8 to
11, it is sometimes contended that the disciples simply spoke,
and that each hearer heard them in his own language. This
would make it a miracle of *hearing* rather than of *speaking*.
Although it sounds attractive at first, this does not fit. It's
clear from verse 4 that they *spoke* in other tongues before

anyone heard them. Besides, who was the Holy Spirit ON, the
speakers or the *hearers*?

Secondly, Philip in Samaria:

> *⁹Now for some time a man named Simon had
> practised sorcery in the city and amazed all the
> people of Samaria. He boasted that he was
> someone great, ¹⁰and all the people, both high and
> low, gave him their attention and exclaimed, "This
> man is the divine power known as the Great
> Power." ¹¹They followed him because he had
> amazed them for a long time with his magic. ¹²But
> when they believed Philip as he preached the good
> news of the kingdom of God and the name of
> Jesus Christ, they were baptised, both men and
> women. ¹³Simon himself believed and was
> baptised. And he followed Philip everywhere,
> astonished by the great signs and miracles he saw.*
>
> *¹⁴When the apostles in Jerusalem heard that
> Samaria had accepted the word of God, they sent
> Peter and John to them. ¹⁵When they arrived,
> they prayed for them that they might receive the
> Holy Spirit, ¹⁶because the Holy Spirit had not yet
> come upon any of them; they had simply been
> baptised into the name of the Lord Jesus. ¹⁷Then
> Peter and John placed their hands on them, and
> they received the Holy Spirit.*
>
> *¹⁸When Simon saw that the Spirit was given at
> the laying on of the apostles' hands, he offered
> them money...*
>
> Acts 8:9-18

This is an important passage, and there are three things to
say. First, the Samaritans were clearly believers (see verse
12) and saved (Mark 16:16). Yet secondly it seems that in
their response to the Gospel, there was something different—
the *power* dimension was missing, perhaps for the first time.
Peter and John added to the ministry by laying hands on the
new converts, "because the Holy Spirit had not yet come upon

any of them, and they received the Holy Spirit." The deficiency was made good. If this is indeed a correct understanding, notice the link again between the *power* dimension and the Holy Spirit coming *upon*. Thirdly, we are not told what tangibly happened or how they knew it, but we *are* told in verse 18 that it was *visible*—Simon *saw* it. His reaction was wrong, but his observation was correct. The importance of this passage is that it indicates a receiving of the Holy Spirit (and I suggest specifically the *power* of the Holy Spirit) subsequent to conversion.

Then we have Peter and Cornelius. Cornelius, a God-fearer, was supernaturally directed to send for Peter who would bring a message through which he and all his household would be saved (see Acts 11:14). In response Peter came and spoke:

> *⁴⁴While Peter was still speaking these words, the Holy Spirit came on all who heard the message. ⁴⁵The circumcised believers who had come with Peter were astonished that the gift of the Holy Spirit had been poured out even on the Gentiles. ⁴⁶For they heard them speaking in tongues and praising God. Then Peter said, ⁴⁷"Can anyone keep these people from being baptised with water? They have received the Holy Spirit just as we have."* Acts 10:44-47

Notice, in verse 44, the Holy Spirit is again said to come *on* them. When Peter recounts this episode to the Church in Jerusalem he says: "As I began to speak, the Holy Spirit came *on* them as he had come *on* us at the beginning." (Acts 11:15, emphasis added.) Linked with this is the observation that they spoke in tongues and praised God.

Fourthly, Paul at Ephesus. But this story starts with Apollos at Ephesus:

> *²⁴Meanwhile a Jew named Apollos, a native of Alexandria, came to Ephesus. He was a learned man, with a thorough knowledge of the Scriptures.*

> *25He had been instructed in the way of the Lord,
> and he spoke with great fervour and taught about
> Jesus accurately, though he knew only the
> baptism of John. 26He began to speak boldly in
> the synagogue. When Priscilla and Aquila heard
> him, they invited him to their home and explained
> to him the way of God more adequately.*
> Acts 18:24-26

For all the learning, something was deficient in the
understanding of Apollos. I suggest that it had to do with the
dimension of the Holy Spirit and power. His understanding
was expanded by Priscilla and Aquila, as a result of which I
would expect him to want to go to Corinth where all the action
was. Sure enough, he wants to go to Achaia, the province in
which Corinth is located.

> *27When Apollos wanted to go to Achaia, the
> brothers encouraged him and wrote to the
> disciples there to welcome him. On arriving, he
> was a great help to those who by grace had
> believed. 28For he vigorously refuted the Jews in
> public debate, proving from the Scriptures that
> Jesus was the Christ.* Acts 18:27,28

So Apollos and the Corinthian Church seemed to be of
mutual benefit to each other. The story continues:

> *19:1While Apollos was at Corinth, [so he indeed
> did go to Corinth] Paul took the road through the
> interior and arrived at Ephesus. There he found
> some disciples 2and asked them, "Did you receive
> the Holy Spirit when you believed?"*

Some people have taken the view that these were not true
Christian believers, but pre-Christians, disciples of John the
Baptist, and that under Paul's ministry here they in fact are
saved. But this view does not stand up to scrutiny. They are
described in verse 1 as "disciples". A study of the Book of
Acts to this point will reveal that the word "disciples", without

further comment, has been used consistently to mean "believers in and followers of Jesus". Why would Luke, the author, suddenly change the use of the term without explanation in this chapter? No, these are followers of Jesus (i.e. Christians), who are in some way deficient in a sense connected with the Holy Spirit, perhaps in a similar way to the believers in Acts 8 before Peter and John laid their hands on them.

> They answered, "No, we have not even heard that there is a Holy Spirit."
> [3]So Paul asked, "Then what baptism did you receive?"
> "John's baptism," they replied.

Does this sound familiar? It's the same language as Acts 18:25. These men must have been the result of the ministry of Apollos, who has naturally reproduced his own shortcomings in those he instructed, before Priscilla and Aquila explained to him the way of God more adequately. Paul sets the men straight.

> [4]Paul said, "John's baptism was a baptism of repentance. He told the people to believe in the one coming after him, that is, in Jesus." [5]On hearing this, they were baptised into the name of the Lord Jesus. [6]When Paul placed his hands on them, the Holy Spirit came on them, and they spoke in tongues and prophesied. [7]There were about twelve men in all.

Note in verse 6, we're told that the Holy Spirit came **on** them, in language linked with power as elsewhere. As a result, they spoke in tongues and prophesied.

These four passages, then, paint a consistent picture. At this stage, we can make four observations:

- Receiving the power of the Spirit is linked to the Holy Spirit coming ON.

- Receiving the power of the Spirit can be at conversion or later.
- Receiving the power of the Spirit is somehow visible.
- Receiving the power of the Spirit is closely linked with speaking in tongues.

This receiving "power from on high" was clearly a feature of the early Church. However as the years became centuries, much of this awareness and experience seems to have been lost, although throughout Church history there have always been groups and individuals who have experienced the power and the gifts of the Holy Spirit. A renewed emphasis came at the beginning of the twentieth century with the Pentecostal revival and the beginning of the Pentecostal Church. It continued throughout the century with the Latter Rain movement, and then the Charismatic movement beginning around 1960, and growing around the world. Liberty Church in Dunfermline was begun in 1979 out of this movement as a charismatic church. The Church's first slogan was "a Charismatic Ministry in Your Community."

My own story is that I learned of the Charismatic movement from books, notably "The Spirit Bade Me Go" by David Du Plessis, and "Nine O'Clock in the Morning" by Dennis Bennett. My investigations became all the more urgent when I discovered to my surprise that I was married to someone who spoke in tongues! I began to seek this empowering experience, but nothing seemed to happen. I found myself looking at other people, people I knew had this experience, and it was as if I could see them wearing a diver's helmet with an oxygen line snaking upwards, like a hotline to heaven. I knew they had something that I didn't have, and I was jealous! After a couple of unsuccessful attempts to meet with someone I thought could help, I knelt down one night by myself at the kitchen table, and asked God to empower me with the Holy Spirit. In line with all the testimonies I had heard, I expected to begin to speak in tongues. So I opened my mouth — but nothing came out. I suppose I expected the Holy Spirit to come upon me, take my voice, and make it say something. At the time, I did not understand that we speak, but the Holy Spirit gives the utterance (see Acts 2:4).

Still nothing seemed to happen that night at the kitchen table. Yet for the next three days, I seemed to feel unusually happy; and a simple old worship song that I didn't even like kept going round and round in my head: "The joy of the Lord is my strength." It was some weeks after this before I spoke in tongues for the first time. However, looking back, I believe I was empowered by the Holy Spirit (that is, that the Holy Spirit came upon me) that night kneeling at the kitchen table.

Does the promise include speaking in tongues? Some people would not be convinced that they had indeed been empowered by the Spirit unless they had spoken in tongues. On the other hand, some people have declined to ask to be empowered by the Spirit, or been hesitant to do so, because they are unwilling to speak in tongues. Both are asking the wrong question. The question is not, "*Must* I speak in tongues?" but rather, "*May* I speak in tongues?" Over the years, speaking in tongues has been a very divisive and much misunderstood gift. Yet it seems very central to the New Testament experience.

Reviewing the Scripture passages, in Acts 2 at Pentecost they clearly spoke in tongues. In Acts 10, they spoke in tongues and praised God, and in Acts 19 they spoke in tongues and prophesied. In Acts 8, there is no direct mention of tongues, but it is clear that some evidence of empowering was perceptible, which Simon saw. It is possible that this was, or included, tongues. One could say, whenever the evidence is specified, tongues is included. In addition, we know that Paul spoke in tongues. He told the Corinthians, "I thank God that I speak in tongues more than all of you." (1 Corinthians 14:18)

Why is it good to speak in tongues? First, it's good because it's *normal*, in the sense that the New Testament knows of no other kind of believer. Secondly, it edifies or builds up the believer (1 Corinthians 14:4). Thirdly, it blesses or praises

God (1 Corinthians 14:16).   Fourthly, it releases prayer (1 Corinthians 14:14,15, and also Romans 8:23,26).

In summary, receiving the power of the Holy Spirit is linked to the Holy Spirit coming ON; it can be at conversion, or later; it comes with evidence or is somehow visible; and it is closely linked with speaking in tongues. Additionally from Acts 8 and Acts 19, we see that the empowering may be appropriated through prayer and the laying on of hands. If we ask, "*Must* I speak in tongues?" the answer is no. But it's better to ask the question, "*May* I speak in tongues?" And the answer to *that* question is apparently yes.

Lastly, don't forget the final key to being clothed with power from on high:

> "*So I say to you: Ask and it will be given to you; seek and you will find; knock and the door will be opened to you. For everyone who asks receives; he who seeks finds; and to him who knocks, the door will be opened.*
>
> "*Which of you fathers, if your son asks for a fish, will give him a snake instead? Or if he asks for an egg, will give him a scorpion? If you then, though you are evil, know how to give good gifts to your children, how much more will your Father in heaven give the Holy Spirit to those who ask him!*" Luke 11:9-13

The final key is: ask.

Printed in Great Britain
by Amazon